THE NATIONAL DIRECTORY OF PSYCHOTHERAPY TRAINING INSTITUTES

Edited by

Laurie A. Baum, M.S.W.
Bette G. Pounds, M.S.W.

BRUNNER/MAZEL *Publishers* • NEW YORK

Library of Congress Cataloging-in-Publication Data
The national directory of psychotherapy training institutes / edited by
Laurie A. Baum and Bette G. Pounds.
p. cm.
Includes index.
ISBN 0-87630-720-9
1. Psychotherapy—Study and teaching—United States—Directories.
2. Psychoanalysis—Study and teaching—United States—Directories.
I. Baum, Laurie A. II. Pounds, Bette G.
[DNLM: 1. Psychotherapy—education—United States—directories.
2. Education, Continuing—United States—directories. WM 22 AA1
N2255 1993]
RC459.5.U6N37 1993
616.89'14'071173—dc20
DNLM/DLC 93-574
for Library of Congress CIP

Published by
BRUNNER/MAZEL, INC.
19 Union Square West
New York, New York 10003

Manufactured in the United States of America

10 9 8 7 6 5 4 3 2 1

Contents

Maryland

Massachusetts

Minnesota

Mississippi

Missouri

New Hampshire

New Jersey

New Mexico

New York

Introduction

WHY READ THIS BOOK?

The National Directory of Psychotherapy Training Institutes is the first comprehensive guide to the diverse psychoanalytic and psychotherapeutic* training institutes based across the U.S.A.

The book was conceived several years ago when the editors finished their own graduate degrees and discovered a multitude of avenues for proceeding with their postgraduate training in psychotherapy. They also found, however, that there was no centralized source of information about these programs. A list of institutes was not even available.

Thus, *The National Directory of Psychotherapy Training Institutes* is a direct response to the void of information about the many freestanding, independent institutes that offer specialized training to psychotherapists, students of psychotherapy, and even nonprofessionals seeking to expand their knowledge

This guidebook lists more than 100 institutes that are freestanding and independent of traditional universities or hospitals. Most of the institutes listed in the directory are small (fewer than 100 students), and information about these institutes is not widely publicized. The directory will, therefore, expose you to many options that you may not have previously considered.

The directory furnishes training information on more than a dozen types of therapies, including Psychoanalysis, Jungian Psychology, Hypnotherapy, Marriage and Family Therapy, Gestalt Therapy, Transpersonal Psychology, Brief Therapy, Cognitive-Behavioral Therapy, Neuro-Linguistic Programming, Adlerian Psychology, Group Therapy, and Mind-Body Therapies. Information on psychotherapy-oriented, degree-granting programs at freestanding institutions is also provided.

* The term *psychotherapist* is used in this book as an umbrella term to denote all professionals, including Psychoanalysts, Psychiatrists, Clinical Social Workers, and Registered Nurses working as Counselors. The term *Psychoanalysis* is used when an institute teaches Freudian Psychoanalysis or an establihed derivative, including Jungian Analytical Psychology. The term *Psychotherapy* is used to refer to other forms of therapy, including those therapies that do not rely on the couch and do not require a minimum of three or four sessions a week.

WHAT THE PROGRAMS CAN OFFER YOU

You may wonder what is behind the proliferation of psychotherapy training programs, and you may be uncertain as to who can attend particular programs and whether that includes you.

Psychoanalytic training was offered to psychiatrists as early as the 1930s, at places such as the New York Psychoanalytic Institute. The first psychoanalytic training institute was established in New York after World War II when a disciple of Sigmund Freud was denied access to a psychoanalytic training institute because he was not a medical doctor. The psychoanalyst, Theodor Reik, founded the National Psychological Association for Psychoanalysis (NPAP) in 1948 and opened its doors to professionals in all fields of study who wished to learn about psychoanalysis.

In subsequent years, as psychoanalytic theory evolved and became more diverse, so too did the institutes, which offered training to practitioners of everything from strict psychoanalysis to alternative forms of psychotherapy.

With no entrance barriers and no formal governing bodies, independent institutes sprang up across the country — although most seem to be based in New York — in mental health clinics, in brownstones, on single floors of obscure buildings, or in founders' apartments.

Nearly half a century later, many psychoanalytic and psychotherapy training institutes are well established, but like the people who practice the profession, many operate quietly behind the scenes. This understated quality of psychoanalytic and psychotherapy training institutes has left many practitioners unaware of the value of engaging in the postgraduate institute-training approach.

Because the process of self-inquiry and the pursuit of higher learning are never ending — and vital to the practice of psychotherapy — some form of continuing education is of crucial importance to practicing psychotherapists.

Institutes expose students to evolving theories and techniques and provide a forum for ongoing dialogue and the exchange of ideas and experiences from the field. This continuing contact with other professionals — be it individual, peer, or group supervision — is invaluable in a field in which many practitioners work on their own. The training institute also offers the psychotherapist an opportunity to share problems and successes, to get feedback, and to develop deeper insights in a spirit of collegiality. This experience enables psychotherapists to continue to grow professionally beyond their formal graduate training.

Institute courses are often open to nearly anyone with an interest in developing his or her psychological awareness. Formal training and certificate programs, however, are generally open to people who have completed their formal degrees and are licensed or certified M.D.s, Ph.D.s, Psy.D.s, M.S.W.s, or R.N.s.

ABOUT THE DIRECTORY

To use this directory you may either turn to the state in which you seek training, where institutes are listed in alphabetical order, or you may turn to the back of the directory, where institutes are grouped according to subspecialties.

The state-by-state institute listings will provide you with a summary of the institute's program, including its psychological orientation, duration, cost, and faculty and class size. Whenever possible, further details such as requirements for classes, case presentations, client caseload, supervision, and personal analysis are included.

We gleaned the names of the institutes included in this directory from every source imaginable — the major accrediting bodies, professional organizations, state departments of education and boards of regents, colleges and universities, other institutes listed in this directory, and telephone books.

Each of the institutes listed in the directory received a questionnaire to elicit the targeted information as well as to determine its status as a freestanding, independent institution that provides ongoing training in psychoanalysis or psychotherapy. Sometimes institutes chose not to answer all questions; therefore, a notation indicates that the information was not provided. Institutes that did not return the questionnaire have not been included in this edition of the directory. However, the participation of all qualified institutes is encouraged, and information on those institutes will be welcome in the second edition of the directory. If you would like your institute to be included in future editions of this directory, please write or fax us at Brunner/Mazel.*

We hope that all readers seeking postgraduate training will find this directory to be an abundant resource in the quest for greater awareness and understanding in the field of psychotherapy.

*Attention Laurie A. Baum, National Directory Update, Brunner/Mazel Publishers, 19 Union Square West, New York, NY 10003; Fax: (212) 242-6339; or fill out and send in the form at the back of the book.

GESTALT INSTITUTE OF PHOENIX

4302 North 32nd Street
Phoenix, Arizona 85018
Telephone: 602 955-9298

Founder(s): Robert Mosby, Ph.D.

Accredited by: American Psychological Association (Category I continuing education)

Affiliated with: None

Psychological Orientation: Gestalt

Duration of Training: 2 years (300 hours) from October to May, plus 1 week in the summer.

Current Tuition: $1230 for the first year, $500 for the summer, and $1350 for the second year

Miscellaneous Fees: $350 room and board for the summer session

Course Fee: $100 nonrefundable deposit (per year)

Seminar Schedule: Weekly Monday night meetings and weekend intensives

Average Class Size: 12

Faculty Members: 11

Annual Applicants: 18

Students Accepted: 12

Enrollment: 12

Graduates: 10

Nonenrolled Students: There are a variety of classes offered for both professionals and nonprofessionals.

Program Admission Requirements:

Candidates must be post-graduates or currently enrolled in a post-graduate course. Candidates must submit an application and have a personal interview.

Program Completion Requirements:

Client Requirements: Not applicable

Personal Analysis: Candidates must have 2 years of group analysis as part of the program.

Supervision Requirements: Candidates receive 28 hours of supervision by faculty members.

Case Presentation Requirements: Not applicable

Thesis Requirements: None

Evaluations: Candidates are required to take an oral exam at the end of the 2-year program.

Additional Information:

Gestalt Therapy is a method of psychotherapy developed in the 1950s by Fritz Perls, M.D. This approach honors each human being as a unique expression of life, living in a culture that may not always allow that uniqueness. The culture itself may have needs that conflict with those of the individual. The artfulness of living is to resolve successfully these conflicts so that both the individual and the culture lived in are nourished.

Each of us has blocks that prevent the free flow of our natural energy. Gestalt Therapy seeks to bring the awareness of the individual, the nature of these blocks, and how they may be dissolved so that the true self may emerge as an ally.

The process of Gestalt Therapy has been applied with success to all types of therapy, including individual, group, marital/couples, family, and children.

MILTON H. ERICKSON FOUNDATION, INC.

3606 North 24th Street
Phoenix, Arizona 85016
Telephone: 602-956-6196/Fax: 602-956-0519

Year Founded: 1979

Founder(s): Jeffrey K. Zeig, Ph.D.

Accredited by: American Medical Association, American Psychological Association, National Board for Certified Counselors

Affiliated with: None

Psychological Orientation: Ericksonian approaches to Hypnosis and Psychotherapy, Brief Therapy

Duration of Training: Varies from 1 day to 14 days for workshops and conferences

Current Tuition: Varies depending on program

Miscellaneous Fees: $5 per hour for archive independent study

Seminar Schedule: Varies

Program Admission Requirements:

Candidates must be professionals in health-related fields who hold master's or doctoral degrees from accredited institutions. Full-time graduate students in health-related fields also are eligible. Previous clinical experience is required for the intermediate and advanced programs. Candidates must meet the Foundation's eligibility requirements.

Program Completion Requirements:

Client Requirements: Not applicable

Personal Analysis: Not applicable

Supervision Requirements: As needed, depending on the course taken

Case Presentation Requirements: Not applicable

Thesis Requirements: None

Evaluations: Newly learned skills are evaluated in the small group practice sessions and supervision that follow lectures.

Additional Information:

The Milton H. Erickson Foundation, Inc. is a federal nonprofit corporation formed to promote and advance the contributions to the health sciences by the late Milton H. Erickson, M.D. The Foundation is dedicated to training health and mental health professionals. Strict eligibility requirements are maintained for attendance at the training events and for receiving the educational materials. The Foundation does not discriminate on the basis of race, color, national or ethnic origin, handicap, age, or sex. Graduate students in the mental health fields are required to submit proof of full-time student status from a regionally accredited institution on letterhead stationery.

To date, the Erickson Foundation has sponsored 5 International Congresses on Ericksonian Approaches to Hypnosis and Psychotherapy, the landmark 1985 and 1990 Evolution of Psychotherapy Conferences, annual seminars, and workshops throughout the United States.

CALIFORNIA FAMILY STUDY CENTER

5433 Laurel Canyon Boulevard
North Hollywood, California 91607-2193
Telephone: 818-509-5959/Fax: 818-762-6547

Year Founded: 1971

Founder(s): Clinton Phillips, Ph.D., and David Jansen, D.Min.

Accredited by: Western Association of Schools and Colleges (WASC)

Affiliated with: None

Psychological Orientation: Family systems

Duration of Training: 2 years for a master's degree

Current Tuition: $340 per credit unit (48 unit program)

Application Fee: $50

Miscellaneous Fees: $100

Course Fee: $550 per semester for case conferences/growth group for first 2 semesters

Seminar Schedule: 11 to 13 units of classroom work per semester, 3 hours of case conference for the first 2 semesters and 45-hour group therapy requirement

Average Class Size: 37

Faculty Members: 12

Annual Applicants: 185

Students Accepted: 120

Enrollment: 250

Graduates: 125

Nonenrolled Students: The Center has a continuing education branch and certificate programs.

Program Admission Requirements:

Candidates must have a bachelor's degree. An orientation interview, 3 letters of recommendation, and a goals essay are required for admission.

Program Completion Requirements:

Seminar Requirements: 48 semester units, a practicum, a thesis, and an oral exam

Client Requirements: Not applicable

Personal Analysis: Not applicable

Supervision Requirements: Not applicable

Case Presentation Requirements: Not applicable

Thesis Requirements: A thesis in the form of a journal article is required.

Evaluations: Information not provided

Additional Information:

The California Family Study Center (CFSC) is a private, nonprofit, freestanding, accredited graduate institution providing an M.A. in Marriage and Family Therapy. CFSC has a full-time enrollment of 250 graduate students. The M.A. program is geared to working adults, and has graduated more than 2,300 students during the past 20 years. The M.A. program blends the latest academic knowledge in the field with a clinical training component and a central personal development focus.

CFSC also offers a Chemical Dependency Studies Certificate Program designed for mental health professionals. This program offers graduate–level education and training in diagnosis, treatment, and prevention of chemical dependency, and offers a certificate to participants of M.A. standing or above who have completed graduate-level work in Marriage and Family Therapy, Social Work, or Psychology. CFSC operates a postdegree clinical training program to serve the local community with marriage and family mental health counseling. The program serves more than 300 individuals, couples, and families per week with affordable (sliding fee scale) counseling.

CALIFORNIA INSTITUTE FOR CLINICAL SOCIAL WORK

2009 Hopkins Street
Berkeley, California 94707
Telephone: 510-528-8422

Year Founded: 1974

Founder(s): Society for Clinical Social Work

Accredited by: State approved

Affiliated with: None

Psychological Orientation: Psychodynamic

Duration of Training: 3 to 6 years

Current Tuition: $7000

Application Fee: $125

Miscellaneous Fees: $200 dissertation binding; $150 graduation fee

Seminar Schedule: Classes meet for approximately 1 full day (Friday or Saturday) every other week. This includes research seminars and clinical colloquium. There are three 3-day convocations per year.

Average Class Size: 8 **Faculty Members:** 14

Students Accepted: 6

Program Admission Requirements:

Candidates must have an M.S.W. degree and a clinical license (L.C.S.W.) or equivalent experience. Candidates must undergo a minimum of 1 year of psychodynamic psychotherapy prior to, or during, the program. Candidates must submit a narrative statement of purpose, 2 clinical case write-ups, and have a personal interview.

Program Completion Requirements:

Seminar Requirements: A minimum of 50 units of class time is required. Candidates must participate in clinical colloquium, research seminars, tutorials with mentors, and clinical practicum.

Client Requirements: A minimum of 3 clients is required.

Personal Analysis: Candidates must have a minimum of 1 year of psychotherapy. Past analysis may be accepted.

Supervision Requirements: Students receive 30 hours of supervision per year for 2 years.

Case Presentation Requirements: Frequent case presentations are required.

Thesis Requirements: The thesis emphasizes qualitative research, however, quantitative studies or theoretical dissertations are welcomed.

Evaluations: Evaluations are conducted by peers, mentors, and clinical supervisors. Integration of theory and practice is emphasized.

Additional Information:

The purpose of the California Institute for Clinical Social Work is to provide educational programs for the professional development and academic advancement of graduate clinical social workers. It offers educational programs comparable in scope and quality to those provided by recognized and accredited institutions of clinical social work education. The purpose of the Ph.D. program is to enable advanced clinicians to integrate theory and to refine practice and research skills for the enhancement of clinical intervention.

The educational philosophy is oriented toward the principle that the aquisition of knowledge is an active process. The adult learner comes to the educational process with her or his own life experience, value system, and learning style. Adults learn best when permitted maximum participation in the process. The ultimate goal of an educational system is to free the individual to pursue his or her own education.

CALIFORNIA INSTITUTE OF INTEGRAL STUDIES

765 Ashbury Street
San Francisco, California 94117
Telephone: 415-753-6100/Fax: 415-753-1169

Year Founded: 1968

Founder(s): Haridas Chadhuri and Bina Chaudhuri

Accredited by: WASC

Affiliated with: None

Psychological Orientation: No specialized orientation/eclectic

Duration of Training: 3 years for those who enter with an M.A. in Psychology and 5 years for those who enter with a B.A./B.S. in Psychology

Current Tuition: $300 per unit

Application Fee: $50

Registration Fee: $50

Supervision Fee: Pay by the unit

Miscellaneous Fees: $200

Seminar Schedule: Quarter system; 3-unit classes meet for a total of 30 hours, usually 2 1/2 hours per week for 12 weeks.

Average Class Size: 20

Faculty Members: 8

Annual Applicants: 153

Students Accepted: 57

Enrollment: 31

Graduates: 18

Nonenrolled Students: Students who are not fully matriculated may take a course as a "Special Student" as long as they have appropriate education that they will be prepared for the specific course they wish to take. Students must complete a "Special Student Application Form" and pay a $25 fee in addition to tuition. "Special Students" may take a maximum of 4 courses; 2 courses in each of 2 quarters.

Program Admission Requirements:

Candidates must have either a B.A./B.S. in Psychology for the Regular Program or a M.A. in Psychology for the Advanced Standing Program. Some volunteer experience is required for the Regular Program; 500 hours of supervised clinical experience is required for Advanced Standing. G.P.A., letters of recommendation, a personal goals statement, an autobiography, an academic paper, and a personal interview are required.

Program Completion Requirements:

Seminar Requirements: Regular Program: 131 units for the Ph.D; 127 units for the Psy.D. Advanced standing: 94 units for the Ph.D., 90 units for the Psy.D.

Client Requirements: During each quarter of practicum, candidates must see 3 clients. After the practicum, students must complete an internship of 1 year or 1500 hours (depending on California licensure requirements). (6 quarters minimum of Practicum are required for Regular, 3 for Advanced.)

Personal Analysis: Personal analysis is encouraged but not required of students.

Supervision Requirements: Candidates must have a minimum of 6 quarters of supervision for the Regular Program, or 3 quarters minimum for the Advanced Standing Program.

Case Presentation Requirements: Not applicable

Thesis Requirements: A dissertation is required.

Evaluations: Information not provided

Additional Information:

The primary objective of the Psychology Doctoral program is to produce competent, well-rounded Psychologists whose practice of Professional Psychology is rooted in a depth of self-knowledge, breadth of world views, and an abiding commitment to honoring and exploring the diverse dimensions of the human experience.

The program is housed in the California Institute for Integral Studies, whose central mission is to provide an environment which emphasizes multidimensional, holistic, and evolutionary perspectives on human existence in order to avoid the fragmentation that has accompanied more traditional academic endeavors.

In an attempt to fulfill this vision, the Psychology Doctoral Program provides rigorous training in the professional practice of Psychology, using the scientist-practitioner model for the Ph.D. student and the practitioner-scholar model for the Psy.D. student.

CALIFORNIA SCHOOL OF PROFESSIONAL PSYCHOLOGY

2749 Hyde Street
San Francisco, California 94109
Telephone: 415-346-4500/Fax: 415-931-8322

Year Founded: 1969

Founder(s): Nicholas A. Cummings

Accredited by: Accrediting Commission for Senior Colleges and Universities of the Western Association of Schools and Colleges. The Ph.D. programs in Clinical Psychology at the Berkeley/Alameda, Fresno, Los Angeles, and San Diego campuses and the Clinical Psy.D. program at the Los Angeles campus are accredited by the American Psychological Association (APA). The Clinical Ph.D. Psychology Program at CSPP-San Diego is in probationary status. The San Diego campus is addressing those issues. The new Psy.D. programs in Clinical Psychology at the Berkeley/Alameda, Fresno, and San Diego campuses have not yet received APA accreditation.

Affiliated with: None

Psychological Orientation: Psychodynamic and Psychoanalytic

Duration of Training: The Clinical Ph.D. curriculum is 5 years. The Organizational Ph.D. and the Clinical Psy.D. curriculums are 4 years.

Current Tuition: $13,180 per year **Application Fee:** $50-$70

Supervision Fee: Varies

Miscellaneous Fees: $150 out-of-state interview

Course Fee: $550 per unit for part-time students

Seminar Schedule: A minimum of 16 academic units per year to a maximum of 22 academic units are required in order to be considered enrolled full-time. Students also devote 8 to 40 hours each week to field placement assignments, including practicum or internships.

Average Class Size: 14 **Faculty Members:** 400

Annual Applicants: 1,400 **Students Accepted:** 480

Enrollment: 2,101 **Graduates:** 270

Nonenrolled Students: CCSP offers a National Continuing Education Program that allows professionals to earn continuing education units.

Program Admission Requirements:

Candidates must either hold or be eligible for an earned B.A. in Psychology from an accredited institution prior to entry, score in the 80th percentile or better on the GRE Advanced Psychology subtest, or have coursework in these 4 areas: Statistics, Tests and Measurements or Differential Psychology, Abnormal Psychology or Psychopathology, and Experimental or Physiological Bases of Behavior or Learning Theory. Clinical experience is preferred, but not required for admission. Candidates must submit an application, transcripts, an essay, and letters of recommendation.

Program Completion Requirements:

Seminar Requirements: The number of seminars varies at each CSPP campus. In the Clinical Psy.D. program, the minimum unit requirement is 106 units and the maximum is 120 units. The minimum unit requirement for students in the Clinical Ph.D. program is 123 units and the maximum is 132 units.

Client Requirements: The number of clients varies depending on placement. Most placements are nonpaying, however, some will offer a small stipend. The campus assists students in finding placements suitable to the students' abilities and interests.

Personal Analysis: Clinical doctoral students (Psy.D. and Ph.D.) are required to have 40 to 45 hours of personal psychotherapy within a 1-year period. The analyst must be a Licensed Psychologist, Licensed Psychiatrist, or Licensed Psychiatric Social Worker. Past analysis is not accepted.

Supervision Requirements: CCSP interns, in both the clinical and organizational Psy.D. and Ph.D. programs, have supervised internships. Placement settings vary. Sites include the Psychological Service Centers (PSCs) established by CCSP, PSC satellite services centers in underserved areas within the campus locale, and specialized service centers, such as the Institute for the Psychology of Women, the Family and Violence Institute, the Anxiety and Stress Disorders Treatment Center, the MERIT Institute, the Ethnocultural Institute, the Youth Gang Consortium, and the Organizational Development Center. Case control will vary with placement setting.

Case Presentation Requirements: Case presentations depend upon the placement setting; most agencies meet weekly to discuss cases.

Thesis Requirements: A thesis is required of students enrolled in the Clinical and Organizational Ph.D. programs. Students in the Clinical and Organizational Psy.D. programs are required to produce a research project or take an examination in conjunction with a doctoral paper and a work sample.

Evaluations: CSPP students are graded on a pass/fail basis. Each campus will evaluate students prior to advancement of doctoral candidacy by oral and written examinations.

Additional Information:

CCSP is the nation's largest graduate school of Professional Psychology. The school is training Clinical and Organizational Psychologists who will broaden and strengthen the roles of psychologists in addressing human need and amelioration of human problems, to serve the needs of our demographically changing society, and combat racism, sexism, ageism, and all forms of discrimination.

C.G. JUNG INSTITUTE OF LOS ANGELES

10349 West Pico Boulevard
Los Angeles, California 90064
Telephone: 310-556-1193/Fax: 310-556-2290

Year Founded: 1954

Founder(s): Professional Society/Southern California Jungian Analysts

Accredited by: State of California, National Association for the Advancement of Psychoanalysis (NAAP), American Boards for Accreditation and Certification, Inc., International Association for Analytical Psychology (IAAP)

Affiliated with: C.J. Jung Institute of San Francisco

Psychological Orientation: Analytical Psychology

Duration of Training: Required 4-year sequence of seminars. Certification is given by a Certification Board (Joint Board/San Francisco and Los Angeles)

Current Tuition: $1750 (preliminary and candidacy stages), $1000 (control)

Application Fee: $150

Seminar Schedule: Classes are held Tuesdays, Wednesdays, Thursdays, or Saturdays, depending on student's selection.

Average Class Size: Information not provided

Faculty Members: Information not provided

Annual Applicants: 10

Students Accepted: 4

Enrollment: 4

Graduates: 2

Nonenrolled Students: The Institute offers "professional seminars" for professionals in the field. There are also open public lectures that anyone may attend. Both professionals and nonprofessionals are permitted to audit a class with the agreement of the instructor.

Program Admission Requirements:

Applicants must have a current license to practice Psychotherapy in the State of California. Candidates must have 200 hours of ongoing analysis with a certified Jungian analyst before applying to the Institute. Candidates must submit 4 copies of the application form, a copy of the college or university transcript where the highest degree was obtained, letters of reference from 3 persons other than past or present analyst(s), a copy of the candidate's professional license, a recent photo (passport size) an application fee ($150) and forms of verification of analytical hours in order to apply for admission into the program.

Program Completion Requirements:

Seminar Requirements: There are 3 stages of training: preliminary stage, candidacy stage, and control stage.

Client Requirements: Candidates must work 3 hours per week with Frantz Clinic or Hilde Kirsch Children's Center patients.

Personal Analysis: Candidates must be in treatment with a Jungian analyst during Institute training; 200 hours of past analysis with a Jungian analyst is required.

Supervision Requirements: Candidates are required to select a control analyst to supervise an analytic case during the final stage of training. The control stage lasts at least 2 years, and candidates must have a minimum of 100 hours of control analysis.

Case Presentation Requirements: Not applicable

Thesis Requirements: None

Evaluations: Final examinations are made to the chairperson of the certifying board of the C. G. Jung Institute of Los Angeles. The control analyst is asked to attest to the completion of the control stage to the certifying board. A trainee is certified as a Jungian analyst by a vote of the joint certifying board, at which time s/he becomes eligible for membership in the C. G. Jung Institute of Los Angeles by a vote of the board of directors. Membership in the International Association for Analytical Psychology is conferred simultaneously.

FAMILY THERAPY INSTITUTE OF SANTA BARBARA

23 West Mission Street
Santa Barbara, California 93101
Telephone: 805-569-2272

Year Founded: 1980

Founder(s): Debra J. Manchester, L.C.S.W., and Gary Meiers

Accredited by: Presently inactive status with the American Psychological Association and the California Medical Association

Affiliated with: None

Psychological Orientation: Integrative Family Systems

Duration of Training: 2 to 3 hours weekly for 8 to 10 weeks

Current Tuition: Information not provided

Course Fee: $300 in advance or $320 if paid in installments

Seminar Schedule: TBA (usually a fall and a summer class, beginning and/or intermediate, determined by student interest)

Average Class Size: 12

Faculty Members: 4

Annual Applicants: 27

Students Accepted: 24

Enrollment: 24

Graduates: 24

Nonenrolled Students: Professionals and nonprofessionals may take classes. Auditing is not permitted.

Program Admission Requirements:

Candidates must be either graduate students or licenced psychotherapists. All skill levels may be admitted, and prior certification is not required.

Program Completion Requirements:

Client Requirements: Not applicable

Personal Analysis: Not applicable

Supervision Requirements: Group and individual supervision are available. Hours may be used toward M.F.C.C., L.C.S.W., or Psychology licensure. Live supervision and/or observation of varied forms of Family Therapy are available through the one-way mirror at the Institute. Videotape feedback is also available for the practicing clinician or intern.

Case Presentation Requirements: Not applicable

Thesis Requirements: None

Evaluations: Information not provided

Additional Information:

The Family Therapy Institute (FTI) offers a complete training program for graduate students and licenced professionals interested in marital and family therapies. All skill levels are addressed—from an introduction to Family Therapy Systems Theory and Therapy to live supervision for therapists already practicing this model.

GESTALT INSTITUTE OF SAN FRANCISCO

P.O. Box 10067
Berkeley, California 94701-5067
Telephone: 510-528-0913

Year Founded: 1967

Founder(s): Fritz Perls, Cynthia Sheldon, Jack Downing, Janie Rayne, Paul Baum, and Abe Levitsky

Accredited by: No accreditation **Affiliated with:** None

Psychological Orientation: Gestalt Therapy

Duration of Training: 2 years **Current Tuition:** $1850 per year

Application Fee: $35

Seminar Schedule: 126 training hours per year, plus 3 weekend intensives per year. 9 day summer intensive each August.

Average Class Size: 10 **Faculty Members:** 7

Annual Applicants: 20 **Students Accepted:** 14

Enrollment: 14 **Graduates:** 7

Program Admission Requirements:

Candidates must be qualified and practicing Psychologists, Psychiatrists, Social Workers, Marriage/Family Counselors, Art, Music and Movement Tterapists, Psychiatric Nurses or Clergy. Candidates also may be presently enrolled as graduate students, with one year of training, or in an internship. Acceptance of allied professionals is determined in the interview process. A personal interview and letters of recommendation are required.

Program Completion Requirements:

Seminar Requirements: 2 years, 126 training hours per year, 3 weekend intensives per year, and 30 hours of individual therapy.

Client Requirements: Not applicable

Personal Analysis: 30 hours of individual Gestalt Therapy are required.

Supervision Requirements: Supervision is included in the training.

Case Presentation Requirements: Not applicable

Thesis Requirements: None

Evaluations: Evaluations are ongoing. Acceptance to second training year is dependent upon the staff's evaluation of the candidate's capacity to participate in, and contribute to, advanced experiential training.

Additional Information:

Gestalt training gives therapists both experience and close supervision in the craft of attending to process. A therapist's capacity for contact, use of self, and empathic recognition of the other are central to the Gestalt approach. Gestalt Therapy teaches both experientially and cognitively. The structure of the program is composed of experiential groups and theoretical presentations that illustrate Gestalt principles. Each year of the 2-year training includes 3 weekend intensives in which trainees have the oportunity to work with the entire faculty. Advanced trainees receive practicum experience in which they work with each other as Gestalt Therapists under faculty supervision. The Institute's aim is ambitious—to produce creative therapists who will integrate the teachings with their individual personalities rather than be obedient or imitative practitioners.

GESTALT THERAPY INSTITUTE OF LOS ANGELES

1460 7th Street, Suite 301
Santa Monica, California 90401
Telephone: 310-319-1663/Fax: 310-319-1663

Year Founded: 1969

Founder(s): Frederic Perls, M.D., Ph.D., James Simkin, Ph.D., Robert Resnick, Ph.D., and Bob Martin, D.S.W.

Accredited by: No accreditation **Affiliated with:** None

Psychological Orientation: Gestalt Therapy, integrating current psychoanalytic and cognitive approaches

Duration of Training: Minimum of 3 years, up to 5 years to complete certification.

Current Tuition: $1300 per year **Supervision Fee:** Arranged

Miscellaneous Fees: $200 certification fee

Seminar Schedule: Minimum of 48 seminar hours per year

Average Class Size: 12 **Faculty Members:** 9

Annual Applicants: 18 **Students Accepted:** 12

Enrollment: 45 **Graduates:** 3

Program Admission Requirements:

A completed degree in a mental health profession such as an M.S.W., M.D., or Ph.D. is required. Prior clinical experience is also required, and will be evaluated on a case-by-case basis. Candidates must attain licensing prior to final certification. The application requirements include an interview, a written application, and letters of recommendation upon request.

Program Completion Requirements:

Seminar Requirements: Candidates must complete 3 years of training, including lectures and experiential work.

Client Requirements: Not applicable

Personal Analysis: Candidates must arrange for therapy with a certified Gestalt Therapist. Frequency and duration are variable. Past analysis may be accepted.

Supervision Requirements: Candidates must arrange for supervision, during which case presentations are monitored.

Case Presentation Requirements: Variable in supervision

Thesis Requirements: None

Evaluations: Candidates are evaluated based on written examinations that cover theory and on live clinical work evaluated by a panel of 3 examiners.

Additional Information:

Gestalt Therapy, as presented at the Gestalt Institute of Los Angeles, treats the whole person within the context of his or her environment. It is a model that uses a comprehensive methodology for integrating a wide range of interventions into a style that suits each individual client and the unique personality of the therapist. The Gestalt Therapy system is grounded in psychoanalytic developmental theory (Freud, Horney, Reich, Sullivan, etc.) and steeped in dialogic existentialism (Buber), within the context of field theory (Lewin). Gestalt Therapy allows the therapist to experiment with, discriminate between, and assimilate ideas and other theories which enliven and enrich our ever-changing approach to psychotherapy.

GROF TRANSPERSONAL TRAINING

20 Sunnyside Avenue, A-314
Mill Valley, California 94941
Telephone: 415-383-8779/Fax: 415-383-0965

Year Founded: 1989

Founder(s): Christina Grof and Stanislav Grof, M.D.

Accredited by: No accreditation

Affiliated with: None

Psychological Orientation: Transpersonal

Duration of Training: 2 years minimum (no maximum)

Current Tuition: $845 per module (7 required) and approximately $200 closing intensive

Application Fee: $50

Seminar Schedule: Requirements: 7 six-day modules (modules offered 2 at a time back-to-back, 4 times per year, closing intensive offered once per year); 150 general hours of Holotropic Breathwork (HB); 10 consultation hours with certified HB facilitators; and closing 2-week intensive.

Average Class Size: 40

Faculty Members: 2

Annual Applicants: 60

Students Accepted: 55

Enrollment: 50

Graduates: 40

Nonenrolled Students: Both professionals and nonprofessionals are permitted to take classes; only previously certified practitioners are permitted to audit classes.

Program Admission Requirements:

A minimum of 5 experiences of HB in workshops with certified facilitators or with the Grofs are required for entry into the program. The application form includes a personal statement.

Program Completion Requirements:

Client Requirements: Not applicable

Personal Analysis: Not applicable

Supervision Requirements: Candidates must have 10 hours of consultation with an HB facilitator.

Case Presentation Requirements: Not applicable

Thesis Requirements: None

Evaluations: Information not provided

Additional Information:

The practice of Holotropic Breathwork is a comprehensive approach to self-exploration that includes and integrates the physical, psychological, and spiritual dimensions. Holotropic Breathwork is a powerful technique of self-exploration and healing, based on and combining insights from modern conscious research, Depth Psychology, and various spiritual practices. The name holotropic (from the Greek holos=whole and trepein=to move in the direction of) means literally "moving toward wholeness." This approach is based on the mobilization of the spontaneous healing potential of the psyche in unordinary states of consciousness, which are induced by breathing and evocative music. Focused body work and mandala drawing are additional important elements used in the holotropic process. In the sessions, participants alternate in the roles of experiencers and "sitters."

Holotropic Breathwork mediates access to all levels of human experience including unfinished issues from postnatal biography, sequences of psychological death and rebirth, and the entire spectrum of trans–personal phenomena.

The theoretical and experiential training in the Holotropic Breathwork is conducted in the bold framework of Transpersonal Psychology, a discipline integrating modern science and the great spiritual traditions of the world. As part of the program, visiting teachers who have done pioneering work in the transpersonal movement explore with participants such areas as shamanism, the Oriental spiritual philosophies, various symbolic systems and maps of consciousness, and psychological aspects of death and dying.

HYPNOSIS CLEARING HOUSE

3702 Mount Diablo Boulevard
LaFayette, California 94549
Telephone: 510-283-3941

Year Founded: 1977

Founder(s): Freda Morris, Ph.D.

Accredited by: California Council of Post-Secondary Education and Vocational Training

Affiliated with: None

Psychological Orientation: Transpersonal and Ericksonian

Duration of Training: 4 months/ 200 hours

Current Tuition: $2,400 **Application Fee:** $50

Miscellaneous Fees: $25 application for tuition loan

Seminar Schedule: 2 weekends per month and 1 Monday per month from 9 A.M. to 8 P.M..

Average Class Size: 13 **Faculty Members:** 3

Annual Applicants: 18 **Students Accepted:** 18

Enrollment: 18

Nonenrolled Students: Both professionals and nonprofessionals may take (but not audit) classes.

Program Admission Requirements:

Candidates must pass a preentrance exam. They must be at least 18 years of age and hold a high school diploma. No prior licensing is necessary, although many candidates are licensed therapists. An application and an entrance exam are required. Interviews are encouraged.

Program Completion Requirements:

Client Requirements: Candidates must have a video practicum.

Personal Analysis: Not applicable

Supervision Requirements: Not applicable

Case Presentation Requirements: Candidates must present 1 video practicum.

Thesis Requirements: None

Evaluations: Information not provided

Additional Information:

The Hypnosis Clearing House training program is designed to insure systematic learning and personal integration of both the science and art of hypnosis. Traditional, Ericksonian, NLP, and Transpersonal approaches are integrated throughout the training to insure that students are familiar with and competent in a variety of therapeutic skills and perspectives. This supports students in developing their own hypnotic style and professional focus. The most significant element of the training at HCH is the emphasis on student experience of the hypnotic process through demonstrations and supervised partner practice. Because graduates understand the transformational effects from the inside out, they are better prepared to help clients move through their inner territories.

INSTITUTE FOR DIALOGICAL PSYCHOTHERAPY

225 Stevens Avenue, Suite 101
Solana Beach, California 92075
Telephone: 619-481-8744

Year Founded: 1984

Founder(s): James DeLeo, Ph.D., Maurice Feldman, Ph.D., and Rich Hycner, Ph.D.

Accredited by: No accreditation

Affiliated with: None

Psychological Orientation: Dialogical

Duration of Training: 2 academic years consisting of 2 training periods of 9 months each (September through May)

Current Tuition: $1170

Seminar Schedule: The 9-month program consists of 3 trimesters. Each trimester consists of 2 semesters that meet on alternate Fridays from 4 P.M. to 6:30 P.M.

Average Class Size: 8

Faculty Members: 3

Annual Applicants: 15

Students Accepted: 8

Enrollment: 8

Graduates: 8

Nonenrolled Students: There is a case-by-case review in which the Institute determines if the individual has special needs or skills.

Program Admission Requirements:

Candidates require a minimum of a year of graduate education and a year of clinical internship. Licensing is preferred, but not required. Candidates must have a personal interview, a group interview, and letters of recommendation.

Program Completion Requirements:

Seminar Requirements: Candidates are required to complete 12 seminars.

Client Requirements: Candidates must conduct a minimum of 5 client sessions per week.

Personal Analysis: Not applicable

Supervision Requirements: Candidates must receive 60 hours of supervision over 2 years.

Case Presentation Requirements: Weekly case presentations are required.

Thesis Requirements: None

Evaluations: Clinical interview evaluations are conducted.

Additional Information:

The Institute for Dialogical Psychotherapy (IDP) arose out of a desire expressed by a number of psychotherapists to apply Martin Buber's philosophy of dialogue—the I-Thou relationship—to the practice of psychotherapy. The Institute presents an approach to psychotherapy and is not a "school" of psychotherapy as such. This approach may apply irrespective of the particular orientation toward therapy or techniques utilized. It rests upon the belief that at the core of human existence is our innerconnectedness with others—the interhuman dimension. Consequently, it is necessary to rethink traditional theories of development, psychopathology, diagnosis, the unconscious, and therapy itself. The focus is on the relational nature of our existence and on reconceptualizing the "self" from within this perspective. The self is not viewed as an isolated self, but is understood within the context of the relational—between person and person. This is not meant to obscure individuality, but rather to place it within the interhuman context.

All "woundedness" is understood within the context of the relational, and psychotherapeutic "healing" is understood as occuring within the context of the therapeutic relationship. While having similarities with a number of other approaches, the dialogical presents a unique philosophy, focus, and context for understanding human interexistence, intersubjectivity, development, "psychopathology," and psychotherapy.

INSTITUTE OF TRANSPERSONAL PSYCHOLOGY

744 San Antonio Road
Palo Alto, California 94303
Telephone: 415-493-4430

Year Founded: 1975

Founder(s): Robert Frager and James Fadiman

Accredited by: Currently in candidacy for accreditation with the Western Association of Schools and Colleges (WASC)

Affiliated with: None

Psychological Orientation: Transpersonal, Psycho-Spiritual

Duration of Training: 4 years for Ph.D.; 3 years for M.A.

Current Tuition: $8100 per year for Ph.D.; $4320 per year for M.A.

Application Fee: $50 **Course Fee:** $180 per unit

Seminar Schedule: 45 units per year for Ph.D.; 24 units per year for M.A.

Average Class Size: 20 **Faculty Members:** 7

Annual Applicants: 90 **Students Accepted:** 74

Enrollment: 50 **Graduates:** 7

Nonenrolled Students: Some classes are open to the general public. No more than 6 units may be taken as a nonmatriculated student.

Program Admission Requirements:

Candidates must have a B.A., preferably in Psychology. If candidate's B.A. is not in Psychology, 12 seminar hours of Psychology courses are required in the Ph.D. program and 8 seminar hours in the M.A. program. Candidates must complete an application, and submit 3 letters of recommendation, transcripts of all schools attended, an autobiography, and a statement of the candidate's relationship to the ITP program. Foreign students must also have TOFEL and credential evaluation.

Program Completion Requirements:

Seminar Requirements: 125 units are required.

Client Requirements: Candidates must complete 750 client hours. In the third year of the Ph.D. program, students work with an advisor and the internship coordinator to develop an internship suited to the experience and interest of the student.

Personal Analysis: Not required, but highly recommended.

Supervision Requirements: Not applicable

Case Presentation Requirements: Not applicable

Thesis Requirements: The Ph.D. program requires a completed dissertation for graduation.

Evaluations: Coursework is evaluated on a pass/no pass basis. Students must complete B-level work or better to pass.

Additional Information:

The mission of the Institute of Transpersonal Psychology is to provide education at the graduate level in Transpersonal Psychology. The Institute's purpose is to prepare students to apply the knowledge, principles, and experiences of Transpersonal Psychology to research, training and the practice of clinicians, counselors, educators and other professionals.

The Institute's broader purpose is to provide leadership in the field of transpersonal psychology. Building on the base of more traditional psychological models and integrating experimental work with theory, the Institute offers residential master's and doctoral programs in Transpersonal Psychology, including a master's degree in Counseling Psychology, an external master's program, and an external certificate program. Through the Transpersonal Counseling Center, the Institute provides psychological assistance to the public-at-large and training to advanced students wishing to pursue a clinical career.

LOS ANGELES INSTITUTE & SOCIETY FOR PSYCHOANALYTIC STUDIES

1100 Glendon Avenue, Suite 933
Los Angeles, California 90024
Telephone: 310-208-3090

Year Founded: 1970

Accredited by: International Psychoanalytic Association, California State Department of Education, Private Postsecondary Division.

Affiliated with: None

Psychological Orientation: Classical Psychoanalysis, Ego Psychology, Object Relations, and Self Psychology.

Duration of Training: 4 years

Current Tuition: $1500 enrollment fee

Application Fee: $125 **Registration Fee:** $60

Supervision Fee: $65

Miscellaneous Fees: Matriculation and graduation

Course Fee: $1500 (16 sessions each)

Average Class Size: Information not provided

Faculty Members: Information not provided

Program Admission Requirements:

Candidates must be licensed mental health care professionals possessing a graduate degree. Candidates must submit a completed application with the fee, transcripts of graduate and undergraduate work, letters of reference, and an autobiography. Personal interviews are also required.

Program Completion Requirements:

Seminar Requirements: 19

Client Requirements: A minimum of 3 supervised cases treated at least 4 times weekly.

Personal Analysis: Personal analysis must start 6 months prior to beginning courses. Candidates are required to choose an analyst from among the training analysts of the Institute. A minimum of 4/week analysis is required.

Supervision Requirements: Candidates must complete at least 200 supervisory sessions. No case may have fewer than 50 supervisory hours.

Case Presentation Requirements: Case conferences are held throughout training. When all other requirements of the Institute are met, candidates must present an analytic case to the Institute.

Thesis Requirements: None

Evaluations: Evaluations of the progress of candidates are made in all phases of the program and are reviewed with the candidate.

MENTAL RESEARCH INSTITUTE

555 Middlefield Road
Palo Alto, California 94301
Telephone: 415-321-3055/Fax: 415-321-3785

Year Founded: 1959

Founder(s): Don D. Jackson, M.D.

Accredited by: No accreditation

Affiliated with: None

Psychological Orientation: Family interactional therapy with families and individuals

Duration of Training: 9 months—shorter programs are available (2 months, 12 weeks, 2 days)

Course Fee: $3000 ($500 due at registration)

Seminar Schedule: Once a week from 1 P.M. to 6 P.M.

Average Class Size: 10

Faculty Members: 2-3

Annual Applicants: 6

Students Accepted: 6

Enrollment: 6

Graduates: 6

Nonenrolled Students: Professionals are permitted to take occasional classes.

Program Admission Requirements:

Candidates must have a background in health or mental health at the bachelor's, master's, or Ph.D. level. Candidates must have prior clinical experience. Prior certification is not required. Application requirements will be discussed on an individual basis with the Program Director.

Program Completion Requirements:

Client Requirements: Not applicable

Personal Analysis: Not applicable

Supervision Requirements: Not applicable

Case Presentation Requirements: Not applicable

Thesis Requirements: None

Evaluations: Students see clients in a 1-way mirror setting, and supervise their own cases.

Additional Information:

The Mental Research Institute has been training professionals from around the world for the last 20 years. MRI does not offer official degrees, so it is a flexible program, providing a very stimulating exchange of ideas. Direct supervision is conducted by the founders of family therapy: John Weakland, Richard Fisch, and a small team of collaborators. Processing of applications is done on a case-by-case basis and often by personal contact with someone in the Institute or the coordinator of the project.

MILTON H. ERICKSON INSTITUTE OF SAN DIEGO

380 Stevens Avenue, Suite 208
Solana Beach, California 92075
Telephone: 619-259-7300/Fax: 619-944-6368

Year Founded: 1984

Founder(s): Michael D. Yapko, Ph.D.

Accredited by: No accreditation

Affiliated with: The Milton H. Erickson Foundation, Phoenix

Psychological Orientation: Brief Therapy approaches

Duration of Training: Variable length workshops

Current Tuition: Varies

Registration Fee: Varies

Course Fee: Varies

Seminar Schedule: Varies. (Schedule is published semiannually.)

Average Class Size: 25

Faculty Members: 1

Nonenrolled Students: Professionals are permitted to take occasional classes.

Program Admission Requirements:

Candidates must be graduate students (M.A. or M.A. equivalent) and above. Candidates must submit an application.

Program Completion Requirements:

Client Requirements: Not applicable

Personal Analysis: Not applicable

Supervision Requirements: Not applicable

Case Presentation Requirements: Not applicable

Thesis Requirements: None

Evaluations: Information not provided

Additional Information:

The Milton H. Erickson Institute of San Diego is an educational center offering training in Clinical Hypnosis and Brief Therapy methods to qualified health professionals. Courses vary from beginning to advanced levels and place emphasis on participants acquiring practical skills in applying methods taught. Course size is limited to maximize learning opportunities.

ROSEN CENTER NORTHEAST

5337 College Avenue, Suite 255
Oakland, California 94618
Telephone: 510-653-9113

Year Founded: 1985

Founder(s): Sue Brenner and Catherine Laroche

Accredited by: Rosenberg Institute, Berkeley, CA

Affiliated with: Rosen Center Southwest, Berkeley, CA

Psychological Orientation: Bodywork, Transpersonal Psychology

Duration of Training: 2 years intensive residential training, 3 times per year, and 2 years internship/advanced training for a total of 4 years.

Current Tuition: $5910 for residential internship and $4010 for internship and advanced training

Supervision Fee: $60 per hour

Seminar Schedule: There are 3 intensives per year (fall, winter, and summer). Each intensive is 8 days long, with 5 hours of training per day.

Average Class Size: 24 **Faculty Members:** 4

Enrollment: 9

Program Admission Requirements:

Candidates must be health care professionals with somatic or psychological training. Personal psychotherapy or bodywork experience is preferred. An interview by telephone or in person, an application, and letters of reference are required.

Program Completion Requirements:

Seminar Requirements: 6 intensives totaling 250 hours and an introductory workshop are required.

Client Requirements: Candidates must see clients for a total of 350 hours during the course of their internships.

Personal Analysis: Students are required to be in ongoing therapy during their internship.

Supervision Requirements: Students must have 30 hours of supervision of 5 cases over a 2-year period.

Case Presentation Requirements: Case presentations are required in connection with the internship during the advanced training.

Thesis Requirements: A final paper on "How you have taken Rosen work into your professional and personal life—have you made it your own?" is required.

Evaluations: Evaluations are ongoing at each level, at the end of the first year, and at the end of the second year.

Additional Information:

The Rosen method is an in-depth, hands-on bodywork/therapy training, using touch as the vehicle to teach participants to reach the healing, essential self. Teaching is offered at residential retreat centers in the New York, Connecticut, and Rhode Island areas. Participants must attend the entire workshop and participate fully. Work is done with participants partially clothed (underpants remain on). Participants will be touching and receiving sessions throughout the training. The training is for psychologically sound individuals.

ROSENBERG-RAND INSTITUTE OF INTEGRATIVE BODY PSYCHOLOGY

1551 Ocean Avenue
Santa Monica, California 90401
Telephone: 310-394-0147/Fax: 310-394-2494

Founder(s): Jack L. Rosenberg, Ph.D., and Marjorie L. Rand

Accredited by: California Board of Post-Secondary Education

Affiliated with: None

Psychological Orientation: Humanistic/Existential, Object Relations, Body Orientation

Duration of Training: There are 3 levels of training. It takes 2 years to receive a letter of completion, 3 years to become a certified practitioner, or 5 years to become certified as a teacher.

Current Tuition: $2000 annually (payable monthly)

Application Fee: $25

Supervision Fee: To be arranged

Miscellaneous Fees: Conference, book, and workshop fees

Seminar Schedule: There are 2 seminar formats: weekly classes (3 are offered at this time), 2 hours per week, and/or 2 weekend groups, that meet 3 days every other month.

Average Class Size: 9

Faculty Members: Information not provided

Students Accepted: 30 **Enrollment:** 30

Graduates: 10

Nonenrolled Students: Professionals may attend one class to observe only.

Program Admission Requirements:

Candidates must have an M.S.W., M.F.C.C., M.A., Ph.D., M.D., or the equivalent in Counseling, Psychology, or a related field. Candidates must be licensed or eligible for licensing. A letter of recommendation and/or a personal interview is required for admission.

Program Completion Requirements:

Seminar Requirements: The basic program is 200 hours, to be taken over 2 years. The Advanced Training Program requires an aditional 100 hours—usually requiring 3 years. Teacher status requires 5 years total.

Client Requirements: Not applicable

Personal Analysis: Candidates must complete 200 hours of Integrative Body Therapy over a 2-year period with an IBP-approved therapist.

Supervision Requirements: Candidates in the Advanced Training Program must receive 100 hours of supervision during the year.

Case Presentation Requirements: Case presentations are required on a weekly basis.

Thesis Requirements: None

Evaluations: Students are evaluated by teachers at the end of each semester. Students fill out evaluations of the teachers and the program each semester. Students must do a live demonstration or a videotape demonstration and pass a written exam.

Additional Information:

Integrative Body Psychotherapy (IBP) combines verbal, cognitive methods with body and breath work to integrate body, emotions, mind, and spirit.

SOUTHERN CALIFORNIA SOCIETY FOR ERICKSONIAN PSYCHOTHERAPY & HYPNOSIS

2101 East 4th St., Suite A1
Santa Ana, California 92705
Telephone: 714-547-8120/Fax: 714-547-5536

Year Founded: 1985

Founder(s): Gary Ruelas, Ph.D., Richard Landis, Ph.D., and Terry Argast, Ph.D.

Accredited by: American Psychological Association, California Board of Registered Nurses, the National Association of Social Workers and NBCC.

Affiliated with: None

Psychological Orientation: Ericksonian Psychotherapy, Systems and Constructivist Models, and General Hypnosis.

Duration of Training: Ongoing programs with modules lasting from a half day to 5 months.

Current Tuition: $50 to $250 per module average

Seminar Schedule: Spring 5-month training (20 hours), spring PTSD/Adult survivor of childhood abuse (20 hours), special population modules (4 hours each), externship supervision (10 hour modules), PTSD/with amnesia training (16 hours)

Average Class Size: 50

Faculty Members: 4

Annual Applicants: 300

Students Accepted: 250

Enrollment: 250

Graduates: Information not provided

Nonenrolled Students: CEUs not manditory

Program Admission Requirements:

Candidates must have a masters degree in a mental health profession or be a student enrolled in an accredited mental health program. Some of the modules offered may require prior clinical experience and prior certification or licensing.

Program Completion Requirements:

Seminar Requirements: Not applicable

Client Requirements: Not applicable

Personal Analysis: Not applicable

Supervision Requirements: Not applicable

Case Presentation Requirements: Not applicable

Thesis Requirements: Not applicable

Evaluations: Not applicable

Additional Information:

SoCSEPH is a privately funded research and training society. Its research focuses on dissociative disorders and on hypnotic phenomena and applications. While it provides clinical supervision throughout Southern California, clinical training seminars are provided throughout the United States and Canada. Members receive a newsletter and special discounts on training seminars and training materials (audio/video tapes and books) and early notification of upcoming programs. The Society's main purpose is the research and dissemination of Ericksonian Psychotherapy and Advanced Hypnosis applications in a social and professional atmosphere.

THE PERSON CENTERED EXPRESSIVE THERAPY INSTITUTE

P.O. Box 6518
709 Davis Street, #106
Santa Rosa, California 95406
Telephone: 707-526-4006

Year Founded: 1983

Founder(s): Natalie Rogers, M.A.

Accredited by: No accreditation

Affiliated with: Sonoma State University, Institute for Transpersonal Psychology, National Expressive Therapy Association, CRAFT

Psychological Orientation: Person-Centered/Transpersonal using the expressive arts (movement, drawing, clay, drama, and writing)

Duration of Training: 400 plus hours

Current Tuition: $3100 plus residency fees

Seminar Schedule: 4 levels: (I) Door to Creativity for 6 days; (II) Creative Self in Community for 9 days; (III) Into the Creative Center for 10 days; (IV) Internship for 22 days

Average Class Size: 25

Faculty Members: 5

Annual Applicants: 55

Students Accepted: 55

Enrollment: 55

Graduates: 7

Program Admission Requirements:

A bachelor's degree is preferred for admission. Candidates must submit a biographical summary.

Program Completion Requirements:

Seminar Requirements: Candidates are required to complete 4 seminars.

Client Requirements: Not applicable

Personal Analysis: Not applicable

Supervision Requirements: Not applicable

Case Presentation Requirements: Not applicable

Thesis Requirements: None

Evaluations: Candidates are required to complete a summary paper and observation notes.

Additional Information:

The Institute offers professional training in Person Centered Expressive Arts Therapy. Experiential courses are offered in residential settings in California, Pennsylvania, and England. The Program is appropriate for learners who want to integrate the arts in a humanistic/transpersonal framework. No prior experience is required; however learners planning to enter private practice should arrange additional training in counseling.

UNIVERSITY FOR HUMANISTIC STUDIES

2002 Jimmy Durante Boulevard
Del Mar, California 92014
Telephone: 619-259-9733/Fax: 619-259-9755

Year Founded: 1977

Accredited by: California State Council for Private Postsecondary Education

Affiliated with: None

Psychological Orientation: Humanistic and Integral M.A., Psy.D., and Ph.D. in Counseling (Clinical), Body-Centered Psychotherapy, and Transpersonal Psychology

Duration of Training: In licensing tracks, 2 years for the M.A. degree, 2 to 3 years for the Psy.D.,and 3 to 4 years for the post-masters.

Current Tuition: $55 per quarter unit for the B.A., $120 per quarter unit for the M.A., and $135 per quarter unit for the Psy.D./Ph.D.

Application Fee: $40

Registration Fee: $160

Miscellaneous Fees: $75 for a comprehensive exam, $100 for graduation

Course Fee: $600 for 5-unit M.A. course, $675 for 5-unit Psy/Ph.D.

Seminar Schedule: Each class meets 48 hours with an instructor who is a licensed, practicing professional holding a terminal academic degree. Depending on the program, the number of classes required range from 17 to 28. Classes meet on evenings and weekends.

Average Class Size: 14

Faculty Members: 9

Annual Applicants: 111

Students Accepted: 75

Enrollment: 205

Graduates: 34

Nonenrolled Students: When there is space available, professionals and non-professionals may audit classes. Auditing students pay $125 for a 2.5-unit class and $250 for a 5-unit class.

Program Admission Requirements:

For the M.A. program a B.A. in Psychology or an equivalent degree is required (prerequisite Psychology classes are available at UHS). For the Psy.D. and Ph.D. programs an M.A. in Psychology or an appropriate field is required. At the B.A. and M.A. level there is no prior clinical experience required, although clinical experience is required as part of the program. Prior certification is accepted, but is not necessary. A personal interview and 2 letters of recommendation are required. An autobiography, a writing competency test, and a general psychology exam are required to determine prerequisites.

Program Completion Requirements:

Seminar Requirements: 85 units (17 classes) plus any prerequisites and a comprehensive exam for the M.A.; 85 to 115 units for the Psy.D. and Ph.D.

Client Requirements: Students must be in internship sites that meet California Board of Behavioral Science and Psychology Board requirements. The University has a University Center for Psychological Services that provides counseling and related services as a low-cost resource to the community. All interns are under direct supervision of a licensed Psychologist who provides individual and group supervision.

Personal Analysis: Candidates must undergo 50 hours of personal analysis during a 3-year period. The psychotherapist must be licensed; no specific orientation is required. If the student has been in therapy during the 2 years prior to being admitted, he or she may request consideration of past hours in therapy by submitting appropriate verification.

Supervision Requirements: Varies with degree

Case Presentation Requirements: Not applicable

Thesis Requirements: None

Evaluations: Information not provided

Additional Information:

The University of Humanistic Sciences degree programs are in Humanistic Psychology and emphasize Counseling Psychology, Health and Body-Centered Psychotherapy, and Transpersonal Studies. Certificate Programs are offered in Addiction Studies and Expressive and Experiential Therapy. Underlying these programs are the assumptions that it is preferable to examine human beings from a holistic, rather than a reductionist, point of view, and that self-examination, social responsibility, and maturation are equal to technique and information as legitimate aims of higher education. The various programs offered at this private nonprofit institution provide opportunities for professional preparation as well as personal enrichment.

VIOLET OAKLANDER INSTITUTE

109 West Mission Street
Santa Barbara, California 93101
Telephone: 805-563-0031

Year Founded: 1989

Founder(s): Violet Oaklander, Ph.D., and Felicia Carroll, M.A.

Accredited by: No accreditation **Affiliated with:** None

Psychological Orientation: A Gestalt Therapy approach to working with children and adolescents.

Duration of Training: 2-week summer intensives and periodic weekend workshops. (2-year training formerly)

Current Tuition: $1200 for a 2-week intensive

Application Fee: $200

Course Fee: Weekend workshop costs vary

Seminar Schedule: Monday thru Thursday 9:30 A.M. to 5:30 P.M.; Friday 9:30 A.M. to 1:00 P.M.

Average Class Size: 24

Faculty Members: 1

Annual Applicants: 68

Students Accepted: 48

Program Admission Requirements:

Candidates must be licensed Psychotherapists or interns working toward licensure. Some advanced students are accepted. Candidates must have experience working with children and/or adolescents. Candidates must submit an application form giving experience, current employment, and education.

Program Completion Requirements:

Client Requirements: Not applicable

Personal Analysis: Not applicable

Supervision Requirements: Not applicable

Case Presentation Requirements: Not applicable

Thesis Requirements: None

Evaluations: Information not provided

Additional Information:

The Violet Oaklander Institute is oriented toward Child and Adolescent Psychotherapy. The training provides an in-depth experience with the therapeutic process developed by Violet Oaklander, Ph.D. The basis of this process is in Humanistic Philosophy and principles of Gestalt Psychotherapy. The Humanistic Philosophy maintains the dignity and worth of each individual and his or her capacity for achieving full potential. Gestalt Therapy is a nonanalytical, noninterpretive form of Psychotherapy concerned with the whole person—body, feelings, intellect, intuitive sense—as well as with awareness and self-acceptence as a prelude to growth and change. Vital to the therapeutic process is the therapist's respect and regard for the child and for the child's experience and viewpoint.

AVALON INSTITUTE

3985 Wonderland Hill Avenue
Boulder, Colorado 80304
Telephone: 303-443-4363

Year Founded: 1986

Founder(s): Charles Bebeau, Ph.D., and Cher Bebeau, M.A.

Accredited by: No accreditation

Affiliated with: Field Faculty for a number of External Degree Programs

Psychological Orientation: Analytic, Jungian, Archetypal

Duration of Training: 1-1/2 to 2 years

Current Tuition: $3600 certificate training

Application Fee: $35 **Registration Fee:** $25

Miscellaneous Fees: $960 training analysis

Course Fee: $400 per course

Seminar Schedule: 9 total: 3 courses per semester, 3 credits each, 3 semesters

Average Class Size: 12 **Faculty Members:** 6

Annual Applicants: 24 **Students Accepted:** 10

Enrollment: 26 **Graduates:** 8

Nonenrolled Students: Professionals and nonprofessionals with some appropriate background may take or audit classes.

Program Admission Requirements:

Candidates must have a B.A. or its equivalent. Prior clinical experience as a therapist or in the healing professions is preferred, but not required. Candidates must have a personal interview and 2 essays on personal history and goals for training.

Program Completion Requirements:

Seminar Requirements: Candidates must complete 9 seminars.

Client Requirements: Not applicable

Personal Analysis: Candidates must complete 24 hours of personal analysis over 1 year with an Analytic, Jungian, or Archetypal therapist. Up to 12 hours of past analysis may be accepted.

Supervision Requirements: Candidates receive 25 hours of supervision over 1 year.

Case Presentations Requirements: Not applicable

Thesis Requirements: A master's-style thesis is required with some applied work presented in case study format.

Evaluations: Written essays, orals at the end of each course, final course papers and thesis orals are required.

Additional Information:

The Avalon Institute blends Carl Jung's original work with more current research into Psychology and the evolution of the soul. The Institute takes Jung's essential concept of the archetype and further develops an understanding of how these collective patterns manifest in human life and mold human personality. Students are introduced to an archetypal perspective through which they can understand the dynamics of their own lives and life in general. These archetypal dynamics offer a way to communicate and understand the language of the unconscious.

In addition to dreamwork and active imagination, the Institute teaches many recently developed body-centered techniques for healing the psyche through the physical aspects of the archetypal process. The Institute has a holistic model for understanding the underlying meaning and for seeing the inherant guidance in physical symptoms, structural issues and organ ailments.

The Avalon Program is structurally designed around three major tracks of learning: Gnosis, Praxis, and Process.

COLORADO CENTER FOR MODERN PSYCHOANALYTIC STUDIES

2240 Linden Avenue
Boulder, Colorado 80304
Telephone: 303 447-0994

Year Founded: 1978

Founder(s): Miriam K. Bloom, M.A., Psy.D., L.F.M.T.

Accredited by: National Association for the Advancement of Psychoanalysis (NAAP)

Affiliated with: None

Psychological Orientation: Psychoanalytic (Modern Freudian)

Duration of Training: Minimum of 6 years

Current Tuition: $175 per course (each course is 3/4 credits)

Application Fee: $25

Registration Fee: $40

Supervision Fee: $250

Miscellaneous Fees: Personal and control analysis

Average Class Size: 8

Faculty Members: 9

Annual Applicants: 4

Students Accepted: 2

Enrollment: 20

Graduates: 4

Nonenrolled Students: Faculty are allowed to audit any class. Others may take parts of workshops for a fee.

Program Admission Requirements:

Beginning candidates must have a bachelor's degree. A master's degree is required to continue beyond 25 classes. Personal analysis is required by the second course and before field work placement. Supervision is required from the beginning of field work. A personal interview is required.

Program Completion Requirements:

Seminar Requirements: Candidates must complete 30 classes at the Psychoanalytic Psychotherapy level and 50 classes at the Psychoanalytic level.

Client Requirements: Candidates must see 2 clients for 1 year each at the psychotherapy level, and 2 clients for 2 years each at the psychoanalytic level.

Personal Analysis: Candidates must complete 400 hours of personal analysis, 100 of which must be with a Modern Freudian analyst. Past analysis may be accepted.

Supervision Requirements: Candidates must receive 150 hours of supervision and complete 6 supervision courses. Candidates must have 1 control case.

Case Presentation Requirements: Case presentations are made informally throughout the training. A final case presentation is required before graduation at the psychoanalytic level.

Thesis Requirements: A journal-quality article is required at the Psychoanalytic Psychotherapist level. A final (dissertation-quality) paper is required at the psychoanalytic level.

Evaluations: Evaluations are ongoing throughout the training program. Teachers meet with directors to discuss the progress of the students.

Additional Information:

The Colorado Center for Modern Psychoanalytic Studies subscribes to the theoretical framework of Sigmund Freud as modified by Hyman Spotnitz. Faced with the limited efficacy of interpretation when dealing with defenses that were learned in the preverbal years, Hyman Spotnitz and other pioneers developed Modern Psychoanalysis as an approach to the resolution of preverbal resistances. As the analyst helps the patient put all his feelings and thoughts into words, the patient's need to confuse his or her mind as a protection of the analyst is gradually given up. Angry and hostile feelings dissipate and the feelings of intimacy and closeness become less threatening.

Modern Psychoanalysts work with the hypothesis that what cures the patient is the resolution of the resistance to saying everything. An important part of the Center's work is to reach out to the community as a whole. Therefore, the Center welcomes professionals and nonprofessionals in the community to its workshops and courses. The center encourages its students to do all or part of their placements in schools or other community organizations.

HARTFORD FAMILY INSTITUTE

17 South Highland Street
West Hartford, Connecticut 06119
Telephone: 203-236-6009

Year Founded: 1969

Founder(s): Stuart W. Alpert, Naomi Bresette, and George W. Rogers, III, Ph.D.

Accredited by: No accreditation

Affiliated with: None

Psychological Orientation: Body-Oriented Gestalt Psychotherapy

Duration of Training: 4, 5, or 6 years

Current Tuition: $1250 per year

Seminar Schedule: 30 evenings (Wednesday nights) approxamately 3 1/2 hours per night from September through June. Two weekend workshops (days only) and a 5-day residential workshop.

Average Class Size: 40

Faculty Members: 4

Annual Applicants: 45

Students Accepted: 40

Enrollment: 40

Graduates: 2

Program Admission Requirements:

Candidates must have a master's degree in mental health or presently attend graduate school. Candidates are expected to be in Body-Oriented Gestalt Psychotherapy. A personal interview is required.

Program Completion Requirements:

Client Requirements: Candidates must have a practice.

Personal Analysis: The decision to accept past analysis is based on a candidate's level of personal integration.

Supervision Requirements: 100 hours of supervision are required over a 1-year period.

Case Presentation Requirements: Not applicable

Thesis Requirements: None

Evaluations: Semiannual peer and faculty evaluations are given.

Additional Information:

The Hartford Family Institute is simultaneously a private practice of 12 Psychotherapists and a training institute with branches in Hartford, Connecticut, Kansas City, Missouri, and Bonn, Germany. The training is rigorous. The criteria for advancement and graduation are subjective. The therapy is intensive, developmental, and existential.

GESTALT INSTITUTE OF CENTRAL FLORIDA

2560 Westminister Terrace
Oviedo, Florida 32765
Telephone: 507-823-2811

Year Founded: 1986

Founder(s): Robert Harman

Accredited by: No accreditation **Affiliated with:** None

Psychological Orientation: Gestalt theory

Duration of Training: 3 years **Current Tuition:** $600 per year

Supervision Fee: $85

Seminar Schedule: Six 2-day weekends per year, 12 hours per weekend.

Average Class Size: 12 **Faculty Members:** 1

Annual Applicants: 15 **Students Accepted:** 12

Enrollment: 11 **Graduates:** 10

Program Admission Requirements:

Candidates must have an M.A., M.S.W., Ph.D., or Ed.D. in an appropriate field or be an advanced graduate student in an appropriate field.

Program Completion Requirements:

Client Requirements: Not applicable

Personal Analysis: Not applicable

Supervision Requirements: Candidates must have 72 hours of supervision over 1 year, including 6 day-long supervision days.

Case Presentation Requirements: 6 case presentations are required.

Thesis Requirements: None

Evaluations: Participants are evaluated subjectively by the director at each meeting and given immediate feedback about their progress, or lack of progress, if that is the case. At the end of each year participants are evaluated to continue in the program.

Additional Information:

Trainees receive a Certificate of Completion upon completing 3 years of training. Trainees participate in groups, theoretical and didactic discussions, supervision, and in dyads and triads. Advanced trainees are expected to lead the group periodically and do individual therapy while the group observes. Training emphasis is upon the application and theory of Gestalt Therapy. Some learning experiences are planned to train therapists to work with children, couples, families, and substance abusers. To finish the program, participants must enroll for 1 year in the advanced supervision.

PSYCHOLOGICAL STUDIES INSTITUTE

2055 Mount Paran Road
Atlanta, Georgia 30327
Telephone: 404-233-3949/Fax: 404-233-6335

Year Founded: 1973

Accredited by: No accreditation

Affiliated with: Georgia State University, Georgia School of Professional Psychology

Psychological Orientation: Christian counseling from an interdenominational, evangelical perspective.

Duration of Training: 2 years to earn a fully accredited master's degree

Current Tuition: $22,000 for Psychological Studies Institute/Georgia School of Professional Psychology, $11,200 (in state) for Psychological Studies Institute/Georgia State University

Application Fee: $20

Miscellaneous Fees: $10 per quarter activities fee

Average Class Size: 30

Faculty Members: 12

Annual Applicants: 80

Students Accepted: 40

Enrollment: 30

Graduates: 29

Nonenrolled Students: The Institute offers some of its classes as audit or nondegree.

Program Admission Requirements:

Candidates must have a 4-year undergraduate degree from an accredited college or university. No prior experience or certification is required. An autobiographical statement, references, a resume, and either GRE or GMAT scores are required for admission.

Program Completion Requirements:

Seminar Requirements: Students must complete M.S. or M.A. requirements through Georgia State University or Georgia School of Professional Psychology along with 32 quarter hours of study through the Psychological Studies Institute.

Client Requirements: At least 90 hours of client contact are required during the 1-year practicum. Students are paid per hour after the 105th hour of client contact.

Personal Analysis: Not applicable

Supervision Requirements: Students participate in weekly supervision while in their practicum.

Case Presentation Requirements: Presentations are done weekly.

Thesis Requirements: None

Evaluations: Information not provided

Additional Information:

The Psychological Studies Institute is a nonprofit educational organization founded to promote training, research, and counseling in the mental health field from an interdenominational, evangelical perspective. The Institute is committed to promoting an understanding of the relationship between Psychology and Theology. The Institute provides a setting where professionals and students with a shared Christian faith join together in studying the integrative application of psychological and theological principles.

The Institute has 2 contractual arrangements: one with Georgia State University and the other with the Georgia School of Professional Psychology. Students who enroll in the PSI/GSU cooperative program earn a M.S. degree in Community Counseling from GSU (this is a fully accredited M.S. degree) and a Diploma in Christian Counseling from PSI. Students enrolled in the PSI/GSPP cooperative program earn an accredited Master of Arts (M.A.) degree in Clinical Psychology from GSPP and a Diploma in Christian Counseling from PSI.

ADLER SCHOOL OF PROFESSIONAL PSYCHOLOGY

65 East Wacker Place, Suite 21
Chicago, Illinois 60601-7203
Telephone: 312-201-5900/Fax: 312-201-5917

Year Founded: 1952

Founder: Rudolf Dreikurs, M.D.

Accredited by: North Central Association Commission on Institutions of Higher Education

Affiliated with: None

Psychological Orientation: Adlerian Psychology

Duration of Training: M.A. Degree Programs and Doctor of Psychology (Psy.D)

Current Tuition: $220 per credit hour

Application Fee: $50

Miscellaneous Fees: $25 student activities fee; $15 library fee

Seminar Schedule: A number of seminars are offered throughout the year.

Average Class Size: 15

Annual Applicants: 153

Students Accepted: 100

Enrollment: 300

Graduates: 8

Program Admission Requirements:

Candidates must have a baccalaureate degree from an accredited institution. Candidates must submit a 500-word autobiography, 2 letters of recommendation, a $50 application fee, all college transcripts, and have a personal interview for the Psy.D. degree.

Program Completion Requirements:

Seminar Requirements: Not applicable

Client Requirements: Not applicable

Personal Analysis: Not applicable

Supervision Requirements: Not applicable

Case Presentation Requirements: Not applicable

Thesis Requirements: Not applicable

Evaluations: Not applicable

Additional Information:

The Adler School of Professional Psychology, founded by Rudolf Dreikurs, M.D., a Viennese Psychiatrist and colleague of Alfred Adler, is a nonsectarian, independent, not-for-profit, coeducational commuter institution. The educational orientation of the Institute is based upon the principles and methods of Individual Psychology, a comprehensive science of living systems originated and developed by the well-known Austrian Psychiatrist, Alfred Adler (1870-1937). Individual Psychology emphasizes the uniqueness of every individual and stresses the individual's relationship with society.

The Adler School is the only accredited, doctoral degree -granting Adlerian Training Institute in the world. The Institute provides instruction, clinical training, counseling, and therapy for individuals, families, and organizations. The School offers degree programs at the doctoral and master's levels, undergraduate and graduate certificate programs, supervised clinical training, a specialization program in Adlerian psychology for professionals, continuing education workshops, and seminars.

The Adler School also maintains a specialized library, a book store, a psychological counseling center, and conducts programs and activites for mental health professionals, students, teachers, and laypersons.

CENTER FOR FAMILY CONSULTATION

820 Davis Street, Suite 221
Evanston, Illinois 60201
Telephone: 708-475-1221

Year Founded: 1977

Founder(s): Carol Moran, M.S.W., Robert Noone, Ph.D., and Sydney Reed, M.S.W.

Accredited by: AAMFT accredited supervision

Affiliated with: None

Psychological Orientation: Bowen Family Systems Theory

Duration of Training: 2 years

Current Tuition: $1900

Application Fee: $50

Seminar Schedule: 20 days, 4 hours per day, for 2 years

Average Class Size: 5

Faculty Members: 4

Annual Applicants: 5

Students Accepted: 5

Enrollment: 5

Graduates: 2

Nonenrolled Students: CFC offers other short-term courses for professionals not enrolled in the training program.

Program Admission Requirements:

Candidates must have a professional degree (M.S.W., Ph.D., M.A., M.Div., M.Ed.). Candidates must have prior clinical experience and current ongoing clinical experience. Certification/licensing is required in candidate's field of practice. Candidates must submit an application form, a family genogram, and have a personal interview.

Program Completion Requirements:

Seminar Requirements: Candidates must complete 3 seminars, 2 workshops, and 2 symposia.

Client Requirements: Candidates must use 5 cases from their own practices as study cases.

Personal Analysis: Not applicable

Supervision Requirements: Candidates receive 30 hours per year of supervision for 2 years.

Case Presentation Requirements: Candidates present cases 2 times each month.

Thesis Requirements: None

Evaluations: Information not provided

Additional Information:

The Center for Family Consultation is an association of family therapists who seek, through research, teaching, and practice, to better understand the emotionally based relationship dynamics of living systems, especially the human family. In addition to the Post-Graduate Training Program, CFC also sponsors the Midwest Symposium, the Fall Conference, research seminars, and monthly consultation groups which focus on particular natural systems - such as family of origin, clinical or work systems. CFC also publishes the "CFC Review".

CENTER FOR PSYCHOANALYTIC STUDY

360 West Erie St.
Chicago, Illinois 60610
Telephone: 312-337-8000

Year Founded: 1985

Accredited by: Illinois Board of Higher Education

Affiliated with: International Federation for Psychoanalytic Education

Psychological Orientation: Psychoanalytic theories of Sigmund Freud, Anna Freud, Heinz Hertmann, Melanaie Klein, Otto Kernberg, Heinz Kohut, Margaret Mahler, Donald Winnicott, and Harold Searles

Duration of Training: 4 to 8 years, 4 years full time.

Current Tuition: $5600 per year

Application Fee: $100

Supervision Fee: $65

Course Fee: $700 per course

Seminar Schedule: Two 3-hour classes, every other Friday for 21 sessions.

Average Class Size: 6

Faculty Members: 9

Annual Applicants: 4

Students Accepted: 3

Enrollment: 14

Graduates: 2

Nonenrolled Students: A student-at-large can take classes without enrolling in the program. The Center occcasionally allows a nonprofessional student to attend selected clesses. The Center recommends that the student work for grades in the event that the student decides to enroll in the certification program or the doctorate program.

Program Admission Requirements:

Candidates must have an M.D, Ph.D., Psy.D., M.A., M.S.W., or an M.S.N. Some clinical experience is preferred. State license and/or certification is necessary, as required by law. Personal analysis is also a requirement for admission. The application includes a personal interview, letters of recommendation, essays, and transcripts of graduate work in a mental health field.

Program Completion Requirements:

Seminar Requirements: 32 courses for the certification of completion in Psychoanalysis. 34 courses for the completion of the doctorate in Psychoanalysis; 2 courses of which are in research method, an original dissertation, and an oral examination.

Client Requirements: At least 2 control cases are required for a minimum of 3 sessions per week. Payment varies.

Personal Analysis: Duration and frequency of individual personal analysis are individually determined.

Supervision Requirements: Candidates must receive 156 hours of supervision of at least 2 control cases during a 2- to 3-year period.

Case Presentation Requirements: Most courses require case presentations; 4 case presentation courses are required.

Thesis Requirements: Candidates must submit a written dissertation consisting of an original contribution to psychoanalysis.

Evaluations: Each student is assigned to a faculty member who guides the student in the planning and evaluation of the academic program. Clinical supervision of control cases entails a sixth-month evaluation, which is repeated on a yearly basis. The evaluation is geared to furthering the self-analytic function of the student, to refining diagnostic skills, creating greater awareness of transference and countertransference, and to developing techniques and clarification of the supervisory role.

Additional Information:

A major focus of the Center's mission is to extend the application of psychoanalysis to include the treatment of severe preoedipal disorders.

CHICAGO CENTER FOR PSYCHOANALYSIS

30 N. Michigan Avenue, Suite 508
Chicago, Illinois 60602
Telephone: 312-443-1099/Fax: 312-372-8738

Year Founded: 1984

Founder(s): Oliver J.B. Kerner, Ph.D., Joanne E. Powers, Ph.D., Johanna K. Tabin, Ph.D., Maurice O. Burke, Ph.D., Kenneth Isaacs, Ph.D., and Irving Leiden, Ph.D.

Accredited by: Incorporated in the State of Illinois as a not-for-profit institution.

Affiliated with: None

Psychological Orientation: Psychoanalytic

Duration of Training: 4 years of full-time academic work and completion of 3 years of supervised psychoanalysis. The average duration is 6 to 7 years.

Current Tuition: Information not provided

Application Fee: $75

Supervision Fee: Variable

Course Fee: Dependent on the number of candidates per course

Seminar Schedule: 9 classes per year (each class including 12 hours of seminar time)

Average Class Size: 8

Faculty Members: 50+

Annual Applicants: 2

Students Accepted: 2

Enrollment: 15

Graduates: 0

Program Admission Requirements:

Candidates must have a Ph.D., M.D., M.S.W., (L.C.S.W. in Illinois), or a Psy.D., as well as 5 years of postdegree clinical experience. Prior certification in the candidate's field is required. Personal analysis is also required. The application requirements include a biographical statement, information on personal analysis, transcripts, curriculum vitae, a copy of a state license, malpractice insurance, and names of professional and clinical references.

Program Completion Requirements:

Seminar Requirements: Candidates must complete 36 credit hours of seminars for graduation.

Client Requirements: Candidates must conduct 3 supervised analyses in continuous treatment for a minimum of 280 45- 0r 50-minute sessions. Patients must be seen at least 4 times a week and they must utilize the couch.

Personal Analysis: Candidates must have a minimum of 1 year of 4 times/week psychoanalysis upon entering the program, and must accrue at least 3 years of psychoanalysis, with a graduate of an accepted and recognized training program. Past analysis is accepted if conducted by a reputable analyst.

Supervision Requirements: Candidates must complete 70 hours of supervision for each of 3 cases. 3 control cases are also required.

Case Presentation Requirements: Depends on individual seminar structure

Thesis Requirements: A final presentation is required. Oral case presentations, a written case summary, a clinical paper, theoretical paper, and empirical research are among the options for a candidate's final presentation.

Evaluations: Supervisory evaluations are done annually, the supervision committee of the center reviews each candidate annually, and the Director of Training meets with each candidate annually.

Additional Information:

The faculty includes or has included Merton Gill, M.D., Fred Pine, Ph.D., Roy Schafer, Ph.D., Donald Kaplan, Ph.D., Joyce McDougall, Ed.D., Ernest Lawrence, Ph.D., Irwin Hoffman, Ph.D., and John Gedo, M.D.

CHILD AND ADOLESCENT PSYCHOTHERAPY TRAINING PROGRAM

180 North Michigan Avenue
Chicago, Illinois 60601
Telephone: 312-726-6300

Year Founded: 1962

Founder(s): Dr. Ner Littner and Esther Schour Zetland

Accredited by: The Institute for Psychoanalysis, of which CAPT is a part, is accredited by the American Psychoanalytic Association. CAPT is not accredited by any formal body.

Affiliated with: Institute for Psychoanalysis, Association of Child Psychotherapists

Psychological Orientation: Psychoanalytic Psychotherapy

Duration of Training: 4 academic years of formal coursework; candidates usually take an additional year to fulfill supervised clinical requirements

Current Tuition: $300 per year

Application Fee: $100

Supervision Fee: $200

Miscellaneous Fees: $100 quarterly administrative fee

Seminar Schedule: 4 1 1/2-hour class meetings per week or Tuesday and Thursday, 8:30 A.M. to 10 A.M., and 10 A.M. to 11:30 A.M.. Program follows the academic year of fall, winter, and spring quarters.

Average Class Size: 10

Faculty Members: 45

Annual Applicants: 15

Students Accepted: 8

Enrollment: 8

Graduates: 4

Nonenrolled Students: Professionals and nonprofessionals may take classes at the Institute for Psychoanalysis.

Program Admission Requirements:

Candidates must have a master's degree in a mental health or human development program. Candidates must have 2 years of supervised experience with children and adolescents. Students are expected to be working in the field prior to, and during, participation in the program. Personal analysis is required for admission—this may be available at a low fee through the Institute clinic. Three interviews, 3 letters of recommendation, transcripts, and a record of work history are required for admission.

Program Completion Requirements:

Seminar Requirements: Candidates must complete an average of 48 courses (10 sessions each) over 4 years.

Client Requirements: Clinical cases are obtained through students' agencies or private practice; some referrals are possible through the Institute.

Personal Analysis: Personal analysis is required for admission. Past analysis is accepted. Analyst's training must be approved by the American Psychoanalytic Association or International Psychoanalytic Association. Verification by analyst that analysis has been completed, or is well under way, is required.

Supervision Requirements: Candidates must be supervised throughout the entire year. Candidates must see 2 cases for 2 years, and 2 for 1 year each, and see 25 supervised diagnostic cases. Frequency of supervision is determined by the needs of the student and the case.

Case Presentation Requirements: No formal requirements other than the regular presentations in the clinical courses, case conferences, and the supervisory process.

Thesis Requirements: None

Evaluations: Students are descriptively evaluated in writing by each course teacher each quarter, by each supervisor on each of the 4 treatment cases, and on each of the 25 diagnostic studies. No letter or pass-fail system of grading is used.

Additional Information:

The objective of the Institute's curriculum is to provide each student with a sound theoretical approach to diagnosis and treatment planning, a body of knowledge of Pychoanalytic Psychology, an understanding of psychotherapeutic techniques for the treatment of children and adolescents and their parents, and the capacity to become teachers, supervisors, and consultants.

The faculty consists of psychoanalytic psychotherapists who are child psychoanalysts and graduates of CAPT. A number of faculty members also have additional specializations within the field of child mental health, such as psychophysiological disorders, childhood schizophrenia, agency and school consultation, and learning disabilities. Occasionally, professionals with specialized knowledge in the field of child mental health are invited to teach as guest faculty.

Students learn to establish a treatment alliance, to understand and effectively utilize transference and countertransference, and to carry psychotherapy through to a conclusion. To facilitate this learning, students are expected to undertake the treatment of 4 cases under faculty supervision. In addition to the 4 treatment cases, 25 supervised diagnostic cases are required.

The Association of Child Psychotherapists is the professional organization of graduates and students of CAPT. The Association sponsors study groups for its members and lectures and conferences for the mental health community. It also supports CAPT through fund-raising events and its scholarship fund for CAPT students.

FOREST INSTITUTE OF PROFESSIONAL PSYCHOLOGY

200 Glendale Street
Wheeling, Illinois 60090
Telephone: 708-215-7870/Fax: 708-215-7912

Year Founded: 1979

Founder(s): Forest Hospital Foundation

Accredited by: North Central Association of Colleges and Universities

Affiliated with: None

Psychological Orientation: The core curriculum is eclectic. Advanced elective courses are offered in Psychodynamic, Cognitive, and Behavioral Therapies.

Duration of Training: Doctor of Psychology Program is 142 credit hours

(Clinical Psychology) and Masters of Psychology Program is 55 credit hours.

Current Tuition: $270 per credit hour

Application Fee: $25

Miscellaneous Fees: $10 activity fee and a $10 liability fee

Seminar Schedule: Full-time and part-time study available.

Average Class Size: 15

Faculty Members: 17

Annual Applicants: 82

Students Accepted: 59

Enrollment: 40

Graduates: 60

Nonenrolled Students: The Institute allows professionals to take occasional classes.

Program Admission Requirements:

Candidates must have a baccalaureate degree with at least 18 hours in psychology for the Psy.D. program and at least 12 hours for the M.A. program. Prior clinical experience is preferred, but not required for admission. Candidates must submit official transcripts, a personal essay, 3 letters of reccomendation, and have a personal interview.

Program Completion Requirements:

Seminar Requirements: Candidates must complete 142 credit hours for the Psy.D. program including a clinical dissertation and internship, and 55 credit hours for the M.A. program.

Client Requirements: Not applicable

Personal Analysis: Not applicable

Supervision Requirements: At least 150 hours of supervision are required over a 2-year period. The number of control cases varies according to the program taken.

Case Presentation Requirements: The number of case presentations required varies according to the program taken.

Thesis Requirements: A clinical dissertation is required for the Psy.D. program; an M.A. paper is required for the M.A. program.

Evaluations: Information not provided

Additional Information:

The Forest Institute of Professional Psychology educates students in the psychological knowledge, skills, and attitudes essential to be effective practicing professional psychologists. It gives students an understanding of human behavior, of the values and methods of scientific inquiry, and of the roles and responsibilities of professional practitioners. The Institute offers 2 graduate degrees: the Psy.D. (Doctor of Psychology) degree in Clinical Psychology, and the M.A. degreee in Psychology.

The Psy.D. program takes 4 years to complete. During the first 3 years, students study theory in psychology and human development; develop skills in psychological assessment, diagnostic testing, and intervention; and participate in supervised clinical practice. The fourth year is devoted to a year-long internship. To graduate, Psy.D. students must complete 142 credit hours, a clinical dissertation, and internship. Part-time study is also available.

The M.A. program offers 5 trimesters of study in the scientific foundations of psychology and human development and 400 hours of supervised clinical training. Its goal is to provide a comprehensive understanding of human behavior and a strong foundation for doctoral studies in clinical psychology. Full- and part-time study are available.

INSTITUTE FOR PSYCHOANALYSIS OF CHICAGO

180 North Michigan Avenue
Chicago, Illinois 60601
Telephone: 312-726-6300

Year Founded: 1932

Founder(s): Franz Alexander, M.D.

Accredited by: American Psychoanalytic Association

Affiliated with: American Psychoanalytic Association

Psychological Orientation: Psychoanalytic

Duration of Training: 6 to 10 years

Current Tuition: $4,300 per year for 5 years, $1000 per year thereafter

Application Fee: $400

Registration Fee: $200

Supervision Fee: $60

Seminar Schedule: 30 classes (approximately 800 hours over a 5-year curriculum

Average Class Size: 7

Faculty Members: 89

Annual Applicants: 8

Students Accepted: 6

Enrollment: 6

Nonenrolled Students: Professionals are permitted to take occasional classes.

Program Admission Requirements:

The Institute requests that prospective candidates inquire directly for details.

Program Completion Requirements:

Client Requirements: Candidates must see 4 cases, 1 terminated, 4 to 5 times weekly, for at least one year. Fees for the first low-fee cases are retained by the Institute. Fees obtained from advanced cases may be retained by the candidate.

Personal Analysis: The training analysis should be conducted at a frequency of 4 or more times a week.

Supervision Requirements: Candidates must receive a minimum of 200 hours of supervision, the cost of which is covered by tuition; 50 hours must be devoted to 2 cases.

Case Presentation Requirements: Not applicable

Thesis Requirements: A thesis is required.

Evaluations: Each candidate receives an annual review by a supervisor. These are reviewed every year by the Institute's Progression Committee.

Additional Information:

The Institute for Psychoanalysis was founded by Dr. Franz Alexander and his first associates, Therese Benedek, Thomas French, Karen Horney, George Mohr, and Helen Ross. The Institute trains individuals in psychoanalytic theory and imbues them with the clinical skills necessary to analyze children, adolescents, and adult patients. The

Institute is devoted to psychoanalysis as a method of treatment, as an ever-growing body of knowledge, and as a set of observations and facts that conceptualize and explain human behavior. The Institute's primary aim is to provide professional training to qualified physicians, psychologists, social workers, and other mental health professionals in the theory and practice of psychoanalysis and to conduct ongoing research in the field.

The Institute has a history of cooperation with other academic and clinical disciplines. It has formed and maintained such prototype programs as the Child and Adolescent Psychotherapy Training Program (CAPT), the Teacher Education Program, and the Barr-Harris Center for the Study of Separation and Loss During Childhood.

Through these diverse educational programs and clinical services, large segments of the general public and a broad range of professional groups involved in interdisciplinary pursuits have benefited. In particular, mental health professionals develop the skills they need to improve the care they offer; scholars have the opportunity to study psychoanalytic theories; and children, adolescents, and adults receive necessary clinical treatment.

In addition to its reputation for cooperating with other academic and clinical disciplines, the Institute has sponsored the establishment of the Cincinnati, Denver, and St. Louis Psychoanalytic Institutes. At present, the Institute is assisting psychoanalytic groups in Milwaukee and Minneapolis-St. Paul.

MILTON H. ERICKSON INSTITUTE OF NORTHERN ILLINOIS

2421 West Pratt Boulevard, Suite 214
Chicago, Illinois 60645
Telephone: 312-274-0746

Year Founded: 1986

Founder(s): Marc Weiss, Ph.D.

Accredited by: Department of Professional Regulation-State of Illinois

Affiliated with: None

Psychological Orientation: Ericksonian, Strategic, Systems, Brief Therapy

Duration of Training: Varies **Current Tuition:** Varies

Supervision Fee: Varies **Course Fee:** Varies

Seminar Schedule: Varies

Average Class Size: 18

Enrollment: 52

Program Admission Requirements:

Candidate must have a master's degree in a health science or must be a full-time graduate student.

Program Completion Requirements:

Client Requirements: Not applicable

Personal Analysis: Not applicable

Supervision Requirements: Not applicable

Case Presentation Requirements: Not applicable

Thesis Requirements: None

Evaluations: Information not provided

THE AMERICAS INSTITUTE OF ADLERIAN STUDIES

600 North McClurg Court Suite 2502A
Chicago, Illinois 60611
Telephone: 312-337-5066

Year Founded: 1980

Founder(s): Robert L. Powers and Jane Griffith

Accredited by: American Psychological Association (approved continuing education sponsor), National Board for Certified Counselors, Personnel Accreditation Institute

Affiliated with: None

Psychological Orientation: The Individual Psychology of Alfred Adler

Duration of Training: 3-course Program for Professionals (3 1/2-day courses)

Current Tuition: $320 per course (seminar costs vary)

Application Fee: $20

Supervision Fee: $100

Seminar Schedule: Three 31/2-day courses in the program for professionals (30 hours each). Seminars on advanced topics are offered over periods from 2 to 5 days, providing from 14 to 37 hours of continuing education credit.

Average Class Size: 14

Faculty Members: 11

Annual Applicants: 156

Students Accepted: 156

Enrollment: 156

Graduates: 29

Program Admission Requirements:

Candidates are required to have a bachelor's degree at the minimum. Most candidates have master's or doctoral degrees. No prior clinical experience is required, but candidates must be actively engaged in the profession at the time of study with AIAS. No licensure or certification is required, though most participants are licensed or certified.

Program Completion Requirements:

Seminar Requirements: Candidates must complete 3 3 1/2-day intensive courses and a paper for each course, demonstrating mastery of course material. Various advanced courses including personality (Adlerian life style) assessment, case consultation seminars, couples therapy, and private Adlerian supervision.

Client Requirements: Not applicable

Personal Analysis: Not applicable

Supervision Requirements: Supervision is offered, but there are no requirements for supervision in the program.

Case Presentation Requirements: Not applicable

Thesis Requirements: None

Evaluations: Information not provided

Additional Information:

The Americas Institute of Adlerian Studies offers comprehensive, short-term training in Alfred Adler's Individual Psychology to those looking for a systematic presentation of Individual Psychology Theory, assessment, and practice. The Program for Professionals in Individual Psychology is also offered in San Diego County (Vista), California. Cooperating local sponsors may arrange to bring the Institute to their locations.

INDIANAPOLIS GESTALT INSTITUTE

9292 North Meridian Street, Suite 311
Indianapolis, Indiana 46260
Telephone: 317-843-0717

Year Founded: 1974

Founder(s): Bob Wagnor, Ph.D., Kay T. Miller, M.S.W., Audrey Savage, Ph.D., Melissa Lawler, M.A., David Phillips, M.D., and David Alexander, H.S.P.P.

Accredited by: No accreditation **Affiliated with:** None

Psychological Orientation: Gestalt

Duration of Training: Basic "2 year" program is 340 hours plus required supervision and individual psychotherapy.

Current Tuition: $4000

Application Fee: $60

Miscellaneous Fees: Residence for training weekends

Course Fee: 11 courses and training materials are included in tuition

Seminar Schedule: 9 weekend seminars for first year (162 hours); 7 weekend seminars for second year (168 hours).

Average Class Size: 20

Faculty Members: 15

Annual Applicants: 34

Students Accepted: 22

Enrollment: 22

Graduates: 19

Program Admission Requirements:

Candidates must have a graduate degree in Psychology or a Human Services field. Candidates must be working in the human services field. Candidates must have a personal interview and submit 3 letters of recommendation and details of past work and medical history for admission.

Program Completion Requirements:

Seminar Requirements: Candidates must complete 16 seminars.

Client Requirements: The number of clients required varies. Candidates receive $200 per month or full payment.

Personal Analysis: Candidates must have a minimum of 10 hours of Gestalt therapy and 50 hours of Gestalt group therapy.

Supervision Requirements: Candidates receive an average of 20 hours of supervision.

Case Presentation Requirements: Candidates must complete 25 hours of Supervised Practicum.

Thesis Requirements: None

Evaluations: Each student is evaluated on his or her growth as a Gestalt Therapist during each session after the fourth session, using peer and staff verbal and written feedback. Year-end comprehensive evaluations by faculty include summary statements of professional competence, personal growth and further potential.

Additional Information:

During the first year basic theory and practice of Gestalt Therapy is taught with primary emphasis on personal growth. Second year seminars include sessions counducted by visiting faculty from other Gestalt Centers in the United States. After completion of the 2-year training, students may apply for faculty internship. Advanced supervision is also available. A certificate of completion is awarded and weekend workshops and groups are offered to the general public. All Indianapolis Gestalt Institute training focuses heavily on personal growth and provides a visceral as well as cognitive understanding of Gestalt Therapy.

NEW ENGLAND INSTITUTE FOR NLP

RFD #3, Pratt Corner Road
Amherst, Maine 01002
Telephone: 413-259-1248

Year Founded: 1982

Founder(s): Richard Clarke, Ph.D.

Accredited by: International Association for Neuro-Linguistic Programming

Affiliated with: None

Psychological Orientation: Strategic Outcome-oriented Therapy, relying upon Ericksonian principles

Duration of Training: Varies: 2-3-day seminars, 12-24-day certification training (divided into 2 to 4 day modules)

Current Tuition: Varies

Supervision Fee: Varies

Miscellaneous Fees: $50 to $100 registration

Course Fee: Varies

Seminar Schedule: Trainings throughout the year (generally a weekend format, some residential)

Average Class Size: 30

Faculty Members: 10

Enrollment: 108

Graduates: 91

Nonenrolled Students: Professionals and nonprofessionals may take classes; previously certified graduates may audit.

Program Admission Requirements:

Candidates are individually assessed depending upon specific program requirements.

Program Completion Requirements:

Seminar Requirements: Attendence at a minimum of 80% of the classes, completion of assigned work, and satisfactory performance in evaluation and testing.

Client Requirements: Varies with program

Personal Analysis: Requirements for personal analysis vary with program.

Supervision Requirements: Requirements vary with the program.

Case Presentation Requirements: Varies

Thesis Requirements: None. Some programs require completion of approved individual projects with written descriptions and oral presentations.

Evaluations: Periodical and final evaluations assessing behavioral competency for each individual are conducted by faculty. Each individual must also demonstrate satisfactory performance in a written examination and oral presentation.

Additional Information:

The New England Institute for Neuro-Linguistic Programming is dedicated to providing the highest quality and most innovative training in NLP in a context of ethical practice and a recognition and respect for the integrity of each person. It offers introductions to and certification trainings in NLP, Ericksonian Hypnosis, and Imperative Self Analysis. It also offers workshops focusing on specialized topics relevant to our roles in today's society, i.e. "Accessing Creativity" and "Stress Reduction Through Multilevel Techniques." The Institute conducts Business and Leadership Seminars, Sales Trainings, and customized Executive Mentoring Programs.

The field of NLP began in the 1970's with an exacting study of several acclaimed experts in communication and change, including Milton Erickson, Virginia Satir, Gregory Bateson, and Fritz Perls. Their strategies and processes were elicited, modeled, and organized into teachable components by Dr. Richard Bandler and Dr. John Grinder as they began the study of subjective experience (NLP). Since then, the field has greatly expanded and extended its investigations, encompassing concepts such as mind-body interconnections and transforming the self.

Through Neuro-Linguistic Programming, experiences in an individual's life which previously had created the illusion of limitation, became opportunities for helping individuals restructure their experience. Behavioral flexibility for both the NLP Practitioner and the client increase in measurable ways, by directing one's experience, rather than being a victim of circumstance. NLP empowers individuals to solution-oriented (not problem) changes, which are ecological, and which release the potential innate in all human beings.

PSYCHOANALYTIC INSTITUTE OF NEW ENGLAND

P.O. Box 762
Needham, Maine 02192
Telephone: 617-449-8365

Year Founded: 1975

Founder(s): Drs. R. Gardner, A. Valenstein, S. Silverman, F. Bonner, H. Tartakoff, G. Bibring, H. Goldings, and M. Stock

Accredited by: American Psychoanalytic Association

Affiliated with: None

Psychological Orientation: Classical Psychoanalysis

Duration of Training: A minimum of 5 to 7 years

Current Tuition: $600 for introductory year, $1200 for years 1 through 5, $4200 for advanced

Application Fee: $100 **Registration Fee:** $100

Supervision Fee: Variable

Seminar Schedule: 10 seminars are offered. Each seminar runs for 2 hours and meets 8 to 16 times during the year.

Average Class Size: 6 **Faculty Members:** 27

Annual Applicants: 4 **Students Accepted:** 3

Enrollment: 22 **Graduates:** 2

Nonenrolled Students: Each person is evaluated individually as to the appropriateness of his or her request and interest.

Program Admission Requirements:

Candidates must have an M.D., Ph.D., M.S.W., Ed.D, or another advanced degree or doctoral level equivalent. Prior clinical experience is individually assessed. Prior certification is required in an appropriate field, by the appropriate Board. Personal interviews, a recent physical exam, letters of recommendation, licensure, and a curriculum vitae are required for admission.

Program Completion Requirements:

Seminar Requirements: 3 seminars of 8 to 16 2 -hour sessions are required.

Client Requirements: Candidates must see a minimum of 3 analytic cases with one in termination phase.

Personal Analysis: Candidates must complete a 4-5-time-a-week training analysis of variable length.

Supervision Requirements: Candidates must have 200 hours of supervision of a minimum of 3 control cases.

Case Presentation Requirements: No minimum

Thesis Requirements: None

Evaluations: Each instructor and supervisor evaluates the candidate twice a year in a written evaluation that is acted upon by the Progressions Committee and the student advisors. Readers also evaluate the case reports, that are submitted every 6 months until termination of the case or graduation of the candidate.

AMERICAN HYPNOSIS TRAINING ACADEMY, INC.

8750 Georgia Avenue, Suite 125E
Silver Spring, Maryland 20910
Telephone: 800-343-9915/Fax: 301-565-0511

Year Founded: 1983

Founder(s): Ron Klein, C.M.C., C.A.A.C., James K. Holwager, and Ph.D., and Kathy Burr, Ph.D.

Accredited by: Maryland State Board of Examiners of Psychologists, New Jersey Academy of Psychology, National Board for Certified Counselors, National Association of Alchoholism and Drug Abuse Counselors, Maryland Addiction Counselor Certification Board, National Academy of Certified Clinical Mental Health Counselors.

Affiliated with: None

Psychological Orientation: Ericksonian Hypnosis, Neuro-Linguistic Programming

Duration of Training: 60 contact hours during 8 days of training

Current Tuition: $850

Seminar Schedule: 2 Thursdays from 12:45 P.M. to 9 P.M.; 2 Fridays, Saturdays, and Sundays from 8:45 A.M. to 6 P.M.

Average Class Size: 50

Faculty Members: 4

Nonenrolled Students: Both professionals and nonprofessionals are permitted to take classes.

Program Admission Requirements:

Candidates must be mental health professionals with graduate degrees or graduate students in mental health programs.

Program Completion Requirements:

Seminar Requirements: 60 hours of seminars must be completed over the 8-day-period (Thursday through Sunday of 2 non-consecutive weeks).

Client Requirements: Not applicable

Personal Analysis: Not applicable

Supervision Requirements: Not applicable

Case Presentation Requirements: Not applicable

Thesis Requirements : None

Evaluations: Information not provided

Additional Information:

This competency-based certification program, intended to enhance the psychotherapeutic training of mental health professionals and addictions counselors, teaches Ericksonian Hypnosis, Neuro-Linguistic Programming, and traditional hypnotic approaches. It meets the demand for an in-depth exploration of the phenomena of hypnosis. This comprehensive 8-day program will lead to certification as a practitioner of hypnosis and will move beyond the introductory patterns of hypnosis to advanced applications. Time will be available to develop and refine trance induction skills, to discover resources leading to rapid and smooth behavioral change for candidates and your clients, and to develop the ability to act effectively.

GESTALT THERAPY CENTER OF BALTIMORE

6117 Benhurst Road
Baltimore, Maryland 21209
Telephone: 410-358-9097

Year Founded: 1986

Founder(s): Rhoda K. Posner

Accredited by: Center for Gestalt Development (The Gestalt Journal)

Affiliated with: None

Psychological Orientation: Gestalt

Duration of Training: 1 year (plus ongoing refresher classes)

Current Tuition: $900

Seminar Schedule: 1 weekend, followed by 6 day-long classes, and a second weekend. There are also daylong workshops and ongoing seminars.

Average Class Size: 8

Faculty Members: 2

Enrollment: 6

Nonenrolled Students: The Gestalt Center allows professionals and some nonprofessionals to take, but not audit, occasional classes.

Program Admission Requirements:

Candidates must have a degree and license in the discipline in which they practice or be in the process of earning a degree. Candidates must be currently practicing. A personal interview is required.

Program Completion Requirements:

Seminar Requirements: Candidates are required to complete 54 hours of seminars.

Client Requirements: Candidates provide their own clients and negotiate payment with them.

Personal Analysis: Not applicable

Supervision Requirements: Not applicable

Case Presentation Requirements: Case presentations are a part of the seminars.

Thesis Requirements: None

Evaluations: Regular feedback is offered, but there are no formal evaluations.

MARYLAND INSTITUTE FOR ERICKSONIAN HYPNOSIS & PSYCHOTHERAPY

6118 Park Heights Avenue
Baltimore, Maryland 21215
Telephone: 410-358-1381

Year Founded: 1989

Founder(s): Hillel Zeitlin, L.C.S.W.

Accredited by: No accreditation

Affiliated with: Milton Erickson Foundation, Phoenix

Psychological Orientation: Ericksonian and related approaches to Psychotherapy, Hypnosis and Therapeutic Communication

Duration of Training: Varies

Current Tuition: Varies

Seminar Schedule: 3 to 4 2-day workshops per year

Average Class Size: Information not provided

Faculty Members: Information not provided

Program Admission Requirements:

Candidates must be at the master's level or above in health or mental health disciplines. Prior clinical experience is necessary. Prior certification is necessary.

Program Completion Requirements:

Client Requirements: Not applicable

Personal Analysis: Not applicable

Supervision Requirements: Not applicable

Case Presentation Requirements: Not applicable

Thesis Requirements: None

Evaluations: Information not provided

Additional Information:

The Maryland Institute for Ericksonian Hypnosis and Psychotherapy provides ongoing supervision and practice groups, as well as workshops, and in-service training utilizing both local and nationally known faculty. The offerings include both beginning and advanced trainings. Past offerings include: "Entrances: Skill Building in Ericksonian Hypnotherapy," "Reclaiming the Self: Solution-Focused Therapy and Ericksonian Hypnosis for Treatment of Adult Survivors of Sexual Abuse," Solution Patterns in Ericksonian Communication," "Soothe Saying: Ericksonian Pain Management," and "Trance Forms: Essentials of Ericksonian Hypnosis. Faculty have included Jeffrey K. Zeig, Ph.D., Yvonne Dolan, M.A., Charles Citrenbaum, Ph.D., Mark King, Ph.D., as well as Institute Director Hillel Zeitman, L.C.S.W.

BOSTON CENTER FOR MODERN PSYCHOANALYTIC STUDIES

1583 Beacon Street
Boston, Massachusetts 02146
Telephone: 617-277-3915/Fax: 617-277-0312

Year Founded: 1973

Accredited by: No accreditation

Affiliated with: None

Psychological Orientation: Modern Psychoanalysis, theories of Sigmund Freud and Hyman Spotnitz

Duration of Training: 5 years, full-time

Current Tuition: $200 per course

Application Fee: $25 **Registration Fee:** $65

Supervision Fee: $275 **Course Fee:** $200

Seminar Schedule: Classes meet 12 times per semester for 1 1/2 hours each. A full-time course load includes four courses and supervision.

Average Class Size: 12

Faculty Members: 18

Annual Applicants: 22

Students Accepted: 21

Enrollment: 78

Graduates: 0

Nonenrolled Students: Professionals and nonprofessionals make take (but not audit) classes.

Program Admission Requirements:

Candidates must complete a master's degree in order to graduate. Once a student is admitted he or she must begin a training analysis. An application, previous educational transcripts, and a personal interview are required for admission.

Program Completion Requirements:

Seminar Requirements: Candidates must complete 40 seminars.

Client Requirements: Not applicable

Personal Analysis: Candidates must complete 300 hours of individual analysis and an additional 150 hours in group or individual analysis with an approved training analyst. Prior analysis is accepted if with an approved analyst.

Supervision Requirements: Candidates must have 50 hours of supervision and one additional control analysis.

Case Presentation Requirements: An oral presentation of a control case and a summary of research findings are required.

Thesis Requirements: A final research project on a control case is required.

Evaluations: P=pass. I=incomplete. NC=no credit. No credit is given to a student who has more than 2 absences. A written evaluation of the student's progress is submitted by the instructor at the end of each course.

Additional Information:

The Boston Center for Modern Psychoanalytic Studies operates on the concept that experiences in utero, and during the preverbal period of infancy, may be relived and transferred to an analyst just as later feeling states are. The patient cannot readily observe and report these early states, just as the infant cannot give verbal information prior to the development of language. Instead, the patient usually reveals fantasies and fears in the form of symptoms and other symbolic communications. These narcissistic transference communications induce feeling states in the analyst, which are used to understand and respond to the patient's experiences. The Center offers two certifications, one as Certified Psychoanalyst, the other as Certified Psychoanalytic Psychotherapist.

BOSTON INSTITUTE FOR PSYCHOTHERAPY, INC.

520 Commonwealth Avenue, Suite 207
Boston, Massachusetts 02215
Telephone: 617-267-1561

Year Founded: 1970

Founder(s): Rutherford Everest, Ph.D., Arthur Forrester, Ph.D., Homer Jernigan, Ph.D., Merle Jordan, Ph.D., James Kirk, Ph.D., Alan Lurvey, Ph.D., Donald Manthei, Ph.D., Richard Moberg, Ph.D., John Reid, Ph.D., Cecil A. Rice, Ph.D., J. Scott Rutan, Ph.D., Louis Schippers, Ph.D., and James W. Smith, Ph.D.

Accredited by: No accreditation

Affiliated with: None

Psychological Orientation: Clinical Fellow Program—a psychodynamic approach to treatment of individuals, couples, and groups. Consultation to organizations.

Duration of Training: 2 years

Current Tuition: Free (Fellows paid a stipend)

Application Fee: $50

Seminar Schedule: 1 1/2-hours per week for 50 weeks per year

Average Class Size: Information not provided

Faculty Members: Information not provided

Annual Applicants: 12 **Students Accepted:** 2

Program Admission Requirements:

Candidates must have a Ph.D. in Psychology, an M.S.W., or an M.D. with a residency in Psychiatry. Considerable prior clinical experience is required, as is prior certification, although exceptions are made in unusual cases. Candidates must submit a form application, transcripts, a personal essay, 3 letters of recommendation, and have 1 or more individual interviews and a group interview.

Program Completion Requirements:

Client Requirements: Candidates must complete 12 to 15 client sessions each week.

Personal Analysis: Long-term psychodynamic analysis is required.

Supervision Requirements: Candidates receive 2 hours of supervision per week.

Case Presentation Requirements: Not applicable

Thesis Requirements: None

Evaluations: Information not provided

Additional Information:

The Boston Institute for Psychotherapy, Inc. was established in 1970 by a group of psychologists who had been trained together at Boston University. The group, believing in the desirability of life-long education, founded a nonprofit organization with a dual purpose: to provide mental health service to the community, and to offer advanced training to mental health professionals who desire to expand their knowledge and skills in psychodynamic psychotherapy.

The Clinical Fellow Programs are for the training of professionals in the treatment of individuals, couples, and groups through a psychodynamic approach. The theories of psychoanalysis are emphasized in the didactic portion of this and all other offerings of the Institute. Other programs of the Institute include the Research Department, the Publications Department, the Center for Effective Organizations, the Treatment Center, Continuing Education, the Organizational Development Program, and the Clinical Consultation Program.

The Institute was born in an atmosphere of collegial fellowship. It strives to maintain that spirit in all of its endeavors. The Institute is an equal opportunity service organization and does not discriminate on the basis of race, color, sex, age, or ethnic origin.

BOSTON CENTER FOR RATIONAL EMOTIVE THERAPY

1101 Beacon Street 6th Floor
Boston, Massachusetts 02146
Telephone: 617-232-9699

Year Founded: 1987

Founder(s): Dr. Robert Heller

Accredited by: No accreditation

Affiliated with: Individual certification in RET available to those associated with the Institute for Rational Emotive Therapy of New York

Psychological Orientation: Rational-Emotive Therapy, Cognitive-Behavioral Therapy, Active, Problem-Focused

Duration of Training: Open-ended

Supervision Fee: $90 per hour

Course Fee: Varies

Seminar Schedule: 3 hours (workshop format)

Average Class Size: Information not provided

Faculty Members: 2

Nonenrolled Students: A variety of workshops are offered to the public and to the professional community. Training/supervision is limited to certified mental health professionals.

Program Admission Requirements:

Information not provided

Program Completion Requirements:

Client Requirements: Not applicable

Personal Analysis: Not applicable

Supervision Requirements: A minimum of 10 hours of supervision are required.

Case Presentation Requirements: Not applicable

Thesis Requirements: None

Evaluations: Written evaluations are available for individuals seeking certification. Supervision in RET is offered at the primary level.

Additional Information:

The Boston Center for Rational Emotive Therapy provides supervision for psychologists seeking licensure in Massachusetts and for mental health professionals seeking training in Rational-Emotive Therapy. The Center provides supervision for affiliates of the Institute for Rational Emotive Therapy of New York who are seeking certification in RET. Supervision by tape or mail is available to individuals in other parts of the state or outside the country. Professional workshops are held through the Massachusetts School of Professional Psychology. Public workshops are held through the Boston Center for Adult Education. The instructor, Dr. Robert Heller, is a postgraduate fellow of the Institute for RET and a certified trainer and clinical supervisor.

KANTOR FAMILY INSTITUTE

7 Shephard Street
Cambridge, Massachusetts 02138
Telephone: 617-868-5450/Fax: 617-868-7811

Year Founded: 1980

Founder: David Kantor

Accredited by: American Association for Marriage and Family Therapy

Affiliated with: Emmanuel College, Andover-Newton Theological Seminary, Lesley College

Psychological Orientation: Family Systems Therapy

Duration of Training: 3 years

Current Tuition: $3,500 per year

Application Fee: $25

Course Fee: $250 per credit hour

Seminar Schedule: 5 to 6 hours per week

Average Class Size: 15

Faculty Members: 43

Annual Applicants: 75

Students Accepted: 74

Enrollment: 50

Graduates: 90%

Program Admission Requirements:

A master's degree or a doctorate is recommended, but candidates with no prior training or experience may be accepted. Current candidates have up to 10 years of previous experience. Prior certification or licensing is not necessary. A personal interview is required.

Program Completion Requirements:

Seminar Requirements: 375 class hours are required over the course of 3 years.

Client Requirements: 500 hours are required

Personal Analysis: Not applicable

Supervision Requirements: 200 hours are needed over the course of 3 years.

Case Presentation Requirements: Every 2 to 6 weeks

Thesis Requirements: Not applicable

Evaluations: Both the trainees and the program are evaluated twice a year.

Additional Information:

The Kantor Family Institute's 3-year Training Program in Family Systems Therapy accommodates a variety of training needs, from an introduction to the field for beginning therapists, to advanced training for professionals with many years of experience. Each stage represents a year of intensive didactic and experiential training in preparation for the next stage, however each can be taken as an autonomous unit. Applicants with prior stage training in Family Systems Therapy enter at the stage that KFI faculty deem most appropriate. Using the Kantor Model as a method of analysis for thinking about Families and Systems

Therapy, KFI has always stood for a "both and" rather than an "either or" approach to systems thinking. Trainees will learn a broad variety of treatment models, including the system and the individual, constructivism and structuralism, and analogic and digital thinking in their clinical models. Clinical placements, individual workshops and courses, joint degree-granting programs with local colleges, and programs in Couples Therapy, Organizational Consultation, Clergy Training, and supervision are also available.

MASSACHUSETTS INSTITUTE FOR PSYCHOANALYSIS

c/o Counseling Center, Tufts University
Medford, Massachusetts 02155
Telephone: 617-627-3360/Fax: 617-627-3019

Year Founded: 1988

Founder(s): Jonathan H. Slavin, Ph.D. and Malcom Owen Slavin, Ph.D.

Accredited by: No accreditation

Affiliated with: Massachusetts Association for Psychoanalytic Psychology

Psychological Orientation: Comparative Psychoanalysis with an emphasis on major current psychoanalytic perspectives

Duration of Training: Regular training program is 2 semesters each year for 4 years. Advanced Candidates training program is 2 semesters each year for 2 years.

Current Tuition: $750 each semester

Application Fee: $130

Supervision Fee: Arranged with the supervisor

Miscellaneous Fees: $200 enrollment fee (advanced candidates)

Seminar Schedule: Tuesdays from 6:30 P.M. to 10:00 P.M. (varies from class to class). Advanced candidates meet every Monday evening from 8:00 P.M. to 10:00 P.M. Classes run from the end of September to the end of May.

Average Class Size: 5

Faculty Members: 30

Annual Applicants: 6

Students Accepted: 4

Enrollment: 18

Graduates: 4

Program Admission Requirements:

Candidates must be either independently licensed in the field of Psychology, Psychiatry, Social Work, or Psychiatric Nursing, or have an interest in Psychoanalysis. Some licensed clinical experience is preferred. Candidates require 3 personal interviews, a personal statement, and letters of recommendation.

Program Completion Requirements:

Seminar Requirements: Candidates must attend 24 seminars.

Client Requirements: Candidates are supervised on 3 cases, 2 of which are psychoanalytic patients treated 4 times a week. Payment is arranged with patients.

Personal Analysis: Candidates must be in personal analysis 4 times per week with a graduate of a recognized institute. Prior analysis may be accepted.

Supervision Requirements: Candidates must receive 200 hours of supervision on the control cases.

Case Presentation Requirements: A Case Conference Seminar is required in all 4 years.

Thesis Requirements: There is no thesis, but a final project is determined by the candidates and the advisory committee.

Evaluations: Evaluations are done in person between the candidates, supervisors, and advisory committee.

Additional Information:

The Massachusetts Institute for Psychoanalysis was formed to offer mental health professionals the opportunity to study psychoanalysis and to be trained to conduct clinical psychoanalysis. The program gives candidates a full sense of the ferment in psychoanalysis today. From the outset, candidates and faculty should have a sense of being part of a living, evolving field of study, a field within which active controversy exists at all levels, from basic assumptions about human nature to clinical theory and methods. This spirit is best conveyed in a comparative psychoanalytic approach that views psychoanalysis in a broad intellectual context and recognizes the existence of several analytic "stances," "modes of listening" or "attitudes," and the assumptions underlying them. Such an approach continually examines what defines psychoanalysis as a specific form of psychotherapy and how it can be usefully modified in work with a wide range of patients, including those with whom couples treatment, family treatment, or medication may be appropriate.

The educational environment stresses a broadly inclusive approach, as well as a true spirit of inquiry which is built around administrative structures and teaching methods that are maximally geared towards open, critical discussion. Students are free to participate in organizing and modifying their own course of study. A spirit of open inquiry and research is seen as an integral part of the candidate's training experience.

SYNTHESIS CENTER

P.O. Box 575
178A Mount Pleasant Street
Amherst, Massachusetts 01004
Telephone: 413-256-0772

Year Founded: 1979

Founder(s): Dorothy Firman

Accredited by: National Association of Social Workers, C.E.U.'s offered

Affiliated with: None

Psychological Orientation: Psychosynthesis, Holistic Counseling, Humanistic and Transpersonal Psychology

Duration of Training: 1, 2, or 3 years

Current Tuition: $2,500 per year

Seminar Schedule: 1 weekend per month for 10 months (131 hours per year)

Average Class Size: 15

Faculty Members: 6

Annual Applicants: 22

Students Accepted: 18

Enrollment: 17 **Graduates:** 12

Program Admission Requirements:

The Synthesis Center considers the relevance of the work to the candidate's background, skills, training, and future plans when considering admission into the program. A personal interview and a brief essay are required.

Program Completion Requirements:

Client Requirements: 3 clients are required at level 3 of the program.

Personal Analysis: Candidates must have 15 hours per year of treatment with a practitioner of Psychosynthesis. Past analysis is accepted if it is recent and appropriate to the student's current needs.

Supervision Requirements: Candidates must have a minimum of 20 hours of supervision.

Case Presentation Requirements: 1 monthly

Thesis Requirements: None

Evaluations: Self evaluations and evaluations done by a 3-person supervision team.

FAMILY THERAPY INSTITUTE, INC.

413 Waconta Street, Suite 500
St. Paul, Minnesota 55101
Telephone: 612-221-1001

Year Founded: 1970

Founder(s): Merle Fossum, A.C.S.W., Rene Schwartz, A.C.S.W.

Accredited by: Continuing Education Units are offered through the College of St. Catherine, St.Paul. Application for accreditation by the Minnesota Board of Marriage and Family Therapy is in process.

Affiliated with: Affiliation with the Minnesota Board of Marriage and Family Therapy is in process. Candidates may be eligible for clinical membership in the American Association for Marriage and Family Therapy.

Psychological Orientation: Family Systems Theory

Duration of Training: 2 years

Current Tuition: $3900 for 2 years

Application Fee: $35

Course Fee: Some workshops require an additional fee.

Seminar Schedule: 1 full day each month 8:30 A.M.to 4:30 P.M. from September to May for 2 years.

Average Class Size: 6

Faculty Members: 11

Annual Applicants: 7

Students Accepted: 5

Enrollment: 5

Graduates: 3

Nonenrolled Students: The Family Therapy Institute offers an extensive program of professional workshops of varying lengths for professionals and others who may be interested.

Program Admission Requirements:

The extern program is open to licensed Social Workers, licensed Marriage and Family Therapists, licensed Psychologists, Psychiatrists, and other Medical Doctors. All professionals are required to have at least a year of full-time clinical work experience. Clinical Counselors, Clergy, School Counselors, Nurses, and others with professional clinical degrees are eligible, but are required to have at least 2 years of clinical work experience. Final selection of applicants will be made by personal interview with the FTI staff.

Program Completion Requirements:

Seminar Requirements: Successful completion of seminars and course(s), if required, presentation of at least 2 observed live family interviews, and demonstration of ability as a family therapist as determined by FTI training staff.

Client Requirements: Not applicable

Personal Analysis: Not applicable

Supervision Requirements: Not applicable

Case Presentation Requirements: Students must present at least 2 observed live family interviews. Students conduct live and videotaped interviews with families.

Thesis Requirements: None

Evaluations: Students must demonstrate their abilities as family therapists to the FTI staff.

Additional Information:

The Family Therapy Institute was incorporated to provide both family therapy and professional training. The ongoing daily involvement in clinical practice exerts a very practical influence upon the training done at the Institute. The workshops are a means of rethinking, gaining perspective, and keeping the clinical work alive.

Some of the training opportunities are designed to help therapists identify family dynamics, understand process, and gain intervention skills. Others are open to any interested individual for learning and personal growth.

MINNESOTA INSTITUTE OF FAMILY DYNAMICS

6950 France Avenue South, Suite 1
Minneapolis, Minnesota 55435
Telephone: 612-927-5499

Year Founded: 1981

Founder(s): Mary Bourne, A.C.S.W. and Dan K. Meyers, A.C.S.W.

Accredited by: No accreditation **Affiliated with:** None

Psychological Orientation: Bowen Theory, The Family Systems (or Natural Systems) Orientation of Murray Bowen, M.D.

Duration of Training: 4 times per year (3 days per quarter). The course is designed for people who come from other parts of the country. The course is designed to be a 3-year course. Some come for 1 year to get acquainted with the theory while others continue training, in some format, for 10 years or more.

Current Tuition: $2000 per year

Application Fee: $25

Supervision Fee: Included in tuition. Advanced supervision is offered for 2 days at a time, 3 times per year, for people who have completed the 3-year program at $150 per day.

Course Fee: $600 for "Family of Origin" local community course

Average Class Size: 14

Faculty Members: 8

Annual Applicants: 30

Students Accepted: 25

Enrollment: 22

Graduates: 9

Nonenrolled Students: Occassionally, when there is a speaker from Georgetown lecturing or for other courses including the 8-session "Family of Origin" class, the class for Ministers, as well as 1-day workshops.

Program Admission Requirements:

The course is open to Therapists, Clergy, Educators, Nurses and Social Workers. Prior clinical experience is preferred but not necessary. An interest in family systems and the ability to understand multigenerational family concepts is desirable. Candidates should be willing to work with their families of origin in supervision sessions and to challenge previous assumptions about the family. Candidates must submit an application, family diagram, descriptive material on their own families, and an essay on the origins of their own theoretical basis for practice.

Program Completion Requirements:

Seminar Requirements: 12 regularly scheduled days (72 hours) per year of direct instruction.

Client Requirements: A trainee is not required to see clients, but rather work with families in a modality and/or setting chosen from a variety.

Personal Analysis: Not applicable

Supervision Requirements: 18 contact hours per year, for 3 years.

Case Presentation Requirements: Quarterly, plus 4 optional sessions during the year. Following the rationale of Dr. Bowen's own training program at Georgetown, most trainees present their own families as cases.

Thesis Requirements: None

Evaluations: Evaluations are based on the ability of the candidate to handle the concepts of Bowen's natural systems theory, to apply them in work with their own families or work systems, and to frame questions and make plans for families that are consistent with theory.

Additional Information:

MIFD was founded to train family therapists from various fields in the use of Bowen Theory. The approach appeals to people who like to solve puzzles, and think of clients as complex personalities embedded in unique processes that have shaped their particular families for generations. The approach is oriented toward the belief that if we can define ourselves more responsibly in our families or work systems, other family members can, indeed, change with us, becoming more flexible, more responsible units and more valuable as concerned support systems.

REFORMED THEOLOGICAL INSTITUTE (MARRIAGE AND FAMILY DEGREE)

5422 Clinton Boulevard
Jackson, Mississippi 39209
Telephone: 601-922-4988

Year Founded: 1966

Accredited by: Southern Association of Colleges and Schools, Association of Theological Schools. The Counseling program is an approved AAMFT Program.

Affiliated with: None

Psychological Orientation: Family Systems

Duration of Training: 2 full years (24 months)

Current Tuition: $1885 for full time students (145 per hour)

Application Fee: $20

Registration Fee: $200

Supervision Fee: $30

Miscellaneous Fees: Graduation and administrative fees

Seminar Schedule: 66 semester hours, taken over a 2-year (24 month) time period. There are 28 courses in the curriculum.

Average Class Size: 20

Faculty Members: 3

Enrollment: 34

Graduates: 17

Nonenrolled Students: Nonmatriculating candidates may take certain courses, however, some courses may not be taken prior to acceptance into the program.

Program Admission Requirements:

Candidates must have a 2.6 GPA for entrance into the seminary. Prior clinical experience is not required. A personal interview, an essay with the application, 3 letters of recommendation, and GREs are required.

Program Completion Requirements:

Client Requirements: Not applicable

Personal Analysis: Not applicable

Supervision Requirements: Candidates must receive a minimum of 100 hours of supervision over a 15-month period and devote 500 hours to control cases.

Case Presentation Requirements: Not applicable

Thesis Requirements: None

Evaluations: Information not provided

FAMILY THERAPY INSTITUTE OF PROVIDENT COUNSEL

2650 Olive Street
St. Louis, Missouri 63103
Telephone: 314-371-6500/Fax: 314-371-6510

Year Founded: 1975

Founder(s): Kathy Lizama, M.S.W.

Accredited by: Commission on Accreditation for Marriage and Family Therapy Education for the American Association for Marriage and Family Therapy

Affiliated with: None

Psychological Orientation: Systemic, Brief, Solution-focused

Duration of Training: 2 year postgraduate training (20 months)

Current Tuition: $2200 per year

Course Fee: $75 workshops

Average Class Size: 8

Faculty Members: 11

Students Accepted: 6-8

Enrollment: 8

Graduates: 6

Program Admission Requirements:

A graduate degree in the marital health field from an accredited program is required. Graduate study should have included human growth and development, personality theory, psychopathology, family systems theory, family studies, research, ethics and professional studies. Additional courses may be required of externs lacking these courses. A minimum of 2 years professional psychotherapy practice, including working with couples and families in a clinic or private setting. A personal interview application form, and 2 letters of recommendation are required.

Program Completion Requirements:

Seminar Requirements: Foundations of Marital and Family Therapy in the first year and Assessment and Intervention in the second year.

Client Requirements: Candidates must have 250 client contact hours on site and 250 client contact hours in an agency or private practice, with a wide range of families.

Personal Analysis: No therapy is required. Recommendations will be made if needed.

Supervision Requirements: Candidates must have 2 hours of a weekly group supervision and 1 1/2 hours of weekly individual supervision over a 20 month period.

Case Presentation Requirements: Weekly audio/video/live case presentations. Live team presentations are made every 4 to 6 weeks.

Thesis Requirements: None. A brief paper is required at the beginning and the end of the program.

Evaluations: Clinical evaluations are done by individual supervisors mid-year and at the end of each year. Coursework evaluations are done by each seminar leader. Externs evaluate faculty after each seminar and evaluate the program at the end of each year. Evaluations are both in-person and written.

Additional Information:

The 2-year postgraduate training in Marriage and Family Therapy for mental health professionals is an advanced training program designed for practitioners who have had a minimum of 2 years of postgraduate clinical experience and who wish to learn systemic models of therapy and to increase their comfort and skill in treating couples and families. The multidisciplinary composition of the externs contribute richness to the learning experience. Externs provide a minimum of 4 treatment sessions per week on site at the Family Therapy Institute. Throughout the program individual supervision is provided in groups of 2 for 1 1/2 hours weekly. Two hours of reflecting team group supervision are provided weekly in groups of 6 students or less. Supervision emphasizes working on individualized learning goals and appreciation of the uniqueness of therapy as "conversational" and "collaborative." Supervisory methods include direct observation of sessions, team involvement in therapy, review of audio and video tapes, along with detailed case discussion utilizing 3-generational genograms. Clinical supervision provides 1 hour of supervision to 5 hours of clinical practice.

The Family Therapy Institute is a part of Provident Counseling, St. Louis' largest mental health organization. The organization has centers located throughout the metropolitan area which include: Central City on Forest Parkway, Clayton Center on Meramec, Crestwood Center on Watson, Illinois Center in Belleville, North County Center on Dunn Road, West County Center on New Ballas Road, and St. Charles Center on Bluestone Drive.

FOREST INSTITUTE OF PROFESSIONAL PSYCHOLOGY

1322 South Campbell Avenue
Springfield, Missouri 65807-1445
Telephone: 417-831-7902/Fax: 417-831-6839

Year Founded: 1979

Accredited by: North Central Association Commission on Institutions of Higher Education

Affiliated with: None

Psychological Orientation: Eclectic

Duration of Training: Full-time for 4 years

Current Tuition: $270 per credit hour

Application Fee: $25

Registration Fee: $200 (Upon acceptance a deposit is required. The deposit is applied to tuition for the first trimester)

Miscellaneous Fees: $150 graduation fee, $80 assessment lab fee

Course Fee: $500 per term for doctoral internship, $250 per term for continuous enrollment (applies to those students who have completed all program requirements but have not completed the oral defense in the PsyD. program)

Average Class Size: 14

Faculty members: 18

Annual Applicants: 41

Students Accepted: 29

Enrollment: 19

Graduates: 14

Nonenrolled Students: Student-at-large status is available for individuals not seeking admission to the program. There is a limit of 12 trimester hours. The 12-credit limit may be waived if the student possesses a doctorate in Psychology and is a licensed Psychologist.

Program Admission Requirements:

Candidates must have a bachelor's degree, 18 hours of undergraduate Psychology, and a 3.25 GPA in the last 60 hours of undergraduate study. Candidates must submit GRE scores, 3 letters of recommendation, official transcripts, and 3 essays, and they must have a personal interview with the admissions committee prior to admission.

Program Completion Requirements:

Seminar Requirements: The curriculum requires 4 years of full-time study which totals 142 credit hours, including practica, internship, and clinical dissertation. Students may attend on a part-time basis; all course requirements are expected to be completed within a maximum of 7 years; 6 practica are required, totaling a minimum of 800 hours.

Client Requirements: A clinical internship of 200 hours or more is completed the final year of the program. Clients are seen throughout practica and internship.

Personal Analysis: Not applicable

Supervision Requirements: All practica and clinical internships are supervised.

Case Presentation Requirements: Requirements for case presentations vary according to individual courses.

Thesis Requirements: Students must present a formal, independent scholarly work representing a contribution to the field. This will involve intensive work with a selected faculty committee plus an oral defense.

Evaluations: Information not provided

Additional Information:

Forest Institute subscribes to the practitioner model of training professional psychologists. The design of the Clinical Psychology Program is based on the belief that a thorough understanding of the comprehensive body of psychological knowledge, skills, and attitudes is essential for professional practitioners. The acquisition of this broad-based understanding and these abilities requires that the curriculum cover a combination of didactic knowledge, skill training, and supervised clinical experience with faculty and supervisors that provide appropriate role models.

FAMILY THERAPY INSTITUTE OF SOUTHERN NEW HAMPSHIRE

Pine Tree Place 360-10A Route
Bedford, New Hampshire 03110
Telephone: 603-472-5740

Year Founded: 1986

Founder(s): Robert Goddard, Ph.D.

Accredited by: Continuing Education Credit for Psychologists (APA), Social Workers (NASW), Mental Health Counselors (NBCC) and EAP Professionals (PDH)

Affiliated with: None

Psychological Orientation: Family Systems Orientation

Duration of Training: 30-week didactic course for 2 hours per week (60 hours)—a prerequisite for the supervision course, 30-week supervision course for 2 hours per week (60 hours), annual spring seminar series

Current Tuition: $900 annual course

Application Fee: $15

Seminar Schedule: 30 2-hour classes

Average Class Size: Information not provided

Faculty Members: Information not provided

Annual Applicants: 20 **Students Accepted:** 15

Enrollment: 15 **Graduates:** 15

Program Admission Requirements:

Candidates must have a master's degree in a related mental health discipline. Prior clinical experience is recommended. Candidates must submit an application form, a resume, and have a personal interview.

Program Completion Requirements:

Seminar Requirements: Introductory Didactic Program or its equivalent, Group Supervision Program, Spring Seminar series. 80% attendance of classes is required. Apprenticeship and Internship Programs are also available.

Client Requirements: Not applicable

Personal Analysis: Not applicable

Supervision Requirements: Not applicable

Case Presentation Requirements: Candidates present cases about once every other week in the Supervision Course.

Thesis Requirements: None

Evaluations: End-of-year evaluations are given, consistent with American Psychological Association guidelines, in order to determine candidates' responses to courses as well as their knowledge base.

Additional Information:

During the past 2 decades, family therapy has emerged as a vital and effective treatment approach for a variety of human problems. The aim of the Family Training Institute is to encourage clinicians to integrate systems thinking into their own clinical style as well as to achieve increasingly sophisticated and creative means for therapeutic intervention.

The evolution of the Psychotherapy field has been a continual process of integration as new theory and research is scrutinized in a manner that enables the therapist to expand clinical skills. The unfolding of Family Therapy and Systems thinking is an important evolutionary step in the exciting process of integrating new concepts and developing new ways to engage in Psychotherapy. Therefore, the aim of the Family Therapy Institute is to provide a forum and a training ground for mental health professionals to expand their current repertoire of clinical skills and clinical understanding. While individual faculty members or presenters may have special areas of expertise and interests, the goal is to provide a complete spectrum of the current field of Systems Therapy.

AMERICAN COLLEGE OF ORGONOMY

P.O. Box 490
Princeton, New Jersey 08542
Telephone: 908-821-1144/Fax: 908-821-0174

Year Founded: 1967

Founder: Elsworth F. Baker, M.D.

Accredited by: No Accreditation **Affiliated with:** None

Psychological Orientation: Biopsychiatric consisting of Psychological and Somatic modalities

Duration of Training: Continuous

Current Tuition: $1,000-3,500 per year depending upon level

Application Fee: $150

Supervision Fee: Hourly fee of supervisor

Seminar Schedule: 3 monthly seminars (1 1/2-hours each); 2 bimonthly seminars (2 hours each).

Average Class Size: 12 **Faculty Members:** 4

Annual Applicants: 2-4 **Students Accepted:** 2

Enrollment: 12 **Graduates:** Not applicable

Nonenrolled Students: Nonmembers occasionally will be allowed to attend seminars, depending on their professional needs.

Program Admission Requirements:

Candidates are required to hold a medical degree plus Board certification in either internal medicine or psychiatry. Candidates must be licensed to practice. Candidates must be in therapy with a training therapist and attend supervisory sessions. Candidates must have a personal interview and submit letters of recommendation.

Program Completion Requirements:

Seminar Requirements: Candidates are required to attend 6 seminars.

Client Requirements: Candidates receive payment for seeing clients bi-annually.

Personal Analysis: Candidates are required to undergo personal analysis with a medical orgone therapist. The frequency and duration of the treatment varies with each candidate. Past analysis is not accepted.

Supervision Requirements: Candidates receive one hour of supervision each week.

Case Presentation Requirements: Case presentations are required 3 to 4 times per year.

Thesis Requirements: Not applicable.

Evaluations: Candidates are evaluated on their performances in the training program continuously to determine if they have the characterological make-up and the knowledge to function as a medical orgonomist.

Additional Information:

The Training Program of the American College of Orgonomy isdedicated to providing trainees with an understanding of the theoretical principles and practice of medical orgone therapy, a form of bio-psychiatric therapy developed approximately 50 years ago by Wilhelm Reich, a disciple of Sigmund Freud. Orgonomic bio-psychiatry integrates a verbal approach through work on the individual character, with body work on muscular problems where behavior is rooted. Focusing on prevention, orgonomy stresses the raising of children in ways that allow them to grow up as free as possible from emotional problems. Dr. Reich appointed Dr. Elsworth F. Baker to continue the work of teaching and training medical orgonomy. Dr. Baker founded the American College of Orgonomy in 1987 to maintain the highest standards in the practice of this form of therapy. This educational program is provided exclusively by board certified licensed psychiatrists.

INSTITUTE FOR PSYCHOANALYSIS & PSYCHOTHERAPY

19B Prospect Street
South Orange, New Jersey 07079
Telephone: 201-762-1553/Fax: 201-762-1553

Year Founded: 1984

Founder(s): Albert Shire, Ph.D., Peter Richman, Ph.D., Louis Brandzel, M.S., A.C.S.W., Judith Felton, Ph.D., Ruth Karr, M.S.W., A.C.S.W., David MacIsaac, Ph.D., and Malcom Marks, Ed.D.

Accredited by: Recognized by the State of New Jersey as a nonprofit educational corporation entitled to grant certificate of completion to its graduates.

Affiliated with: None

Psychological Orientation: Freudian, Ego-Psychology, Object-Relations, Self Psychology

Duration of Training: 3-year program in Psychoanalytic Psychotherapy; an additional 3 years for certificate of completion in Psychoanalysis

Current Tuition: Information not provided

Application Fee: $25

Registration Fee: $35

Supervision Fee: Each

Miscellaneous Fees: $25 student dues

Course Fee: $265

Seminar Schedule: Two 1 1/2-hour courses for a 15 week semester, 6 semesters in the first 3 years and 6 semesters in the second 3 years.

Average Class Size: 6

Faculty Members: 46

Annual Applicants: 28

Students Accepted: 21

Enrollment: 74

Graduates: 23

Nonenrolled Students: Professionals are permitted to audit or take first year classes.

Program Admission Requirements:

Candidates must have, or be eligible for, legal entitlement or licensure to practice Psychotherapy independently in a recognized mental health profession. It is the Institute's understanding of N.J. law that the independent practice of Psychotherapy is currently restricted to Social Workers, Licenced Psychologists, Psychiatrists, Psychiatric Nurses, and Pastoral Counselors. Incoming students must have 150 hours of prior clinical experience. One patient should be seen for 50 hours and 1 for 100 hours. An application interview is required.

Program Completion Requirements:

Seminar Requirements: 12 seminars in the first 3 years and 12 seminars in the second 3 years are required. Candidates may apply for advanced standing if they possess special qualifications, thereby reducing some of the requirements. In order to obtain advanced standing, the prospective candidate must make a case presentation to a committee consisting of 3 members of the Training Committee.

*Client Requirements:*Readiness for control psychoanalysis students must have a minimum of 300 patient hours with at least 3 patients. Final case presentation Psychotherapy students must have 2 separate patients 3 times per week with a minimum of 50 hours each. One client must be ongoing for a minimum of 2 years. Incoming students must have 150 hours--1 patient at 50 hours and 1 at 100 hours.

Personal Analysis: Candidates for a Psychotherapy Certificate must have 250 hours of personal analysis, and candidates for a Psychoanalysis Certificate must have 400 hours of personal analysis with an analyst who has had either a Freudian analysis or a Freudian control.

Supervision Requirements: For completion of the training program in Psychotherapy, candidates must complete 2 periods of intensive supervision for a minimum of 50 hours each with 2 different IPPNJ analysts. For completion of the Psychoanalysis Program, 2 additional periods of intensive supervision are required, 1 comprising a minimum of 50 meetings, the other of 100 meetings, with 2 different IPPNJ analysts.

Case Presentation Requirements: All IPPNJ courses require of each participant either a paper or an oral presentation. At the end of the first 3 years students make a case presentation to obtain their certificates of completion of study and supervision in Psychoanalytic Psychotherapy. At the end of the subsequent 3 years, the candidate makes a final case presentation to obtain certification of completion of study and supervised work in Psychoanalysis.

Thesis Requirements: None

Evaluations: After each semester, each instructor writes subjective evaluations. In addition, students are rated on a scale of 1 to 5 on different items reflecting their abilities and talents. Instructors are similarly evaluated by students.

MILTON H. ERICKSON INSTITUTE OF NEW JERSEY

20 Nassau Street
Princeton, New Jersey 08540
Telephone: 609-924-2508

Year Founded: 1991

Founder(s): Harriet E. Hollander, Ph.D.

Accredited by: Milton H. Erickson Foundation, Phoenix

Affiliated with: Milton H. Erickson Foundation, Phoenix

Psychological Orientation: Ericksonian approaches to psychotherapy

Duration of Training: 2-day introductory course; First-year course totals 52 hours and second year requires supervision in small groups and monthly 2-hour sessions.

Current Tuition: $165 for 2-day courses and $1300 for year courses

Supervision Fee: Approximately $60 per hour for supervision in groups of 4

Seminar Schedule: First-year course meets Tuesday for 2 hours from October to April

Average Class Size: 18 **Faculty Members:** 1

Annual Applicants: 18

Program Admission Requirements:

Candidates must have a Ph.D., M.D., M.S.W., or the equivalent. Candidates must be licensed. Supervised clinical experience in an accredited program is required. The year course requires introductory work and the permission of the director.

Program Completion Requirements:

Seminar Requirements: Candidates must attend classes for the first year to meet eligibility requirements for membership in the American Society of Clinical Hypnosis.

Client Requirements: Not applicable

Personal Analysis: Not applicable

Supervision Requirements: Not applicable

Case Presentation Requirements: Not applicable

Thesis Requirements: None

Evaluations: Information not provided

Additional Information:

The Milton H. Erickson Institute of New Jersey is associated with the Milton H. Erickson Foundation, Inc. of Phoenix and follows the Foundation's general guidelines. The Institute provides educational programs in Clinical Hypnotherapy and Psychotherapy for Physicians, Dentists, Psychologists, Social Workers, and other mental health professionals from accredited programs eligible for licensing in the state. Workshops are offered at the introductory, intermediate, and advanced levels of training. A year-long course in integration of Ericksonian approaches into Psychotherapy is offered. Supervision groups for the second level of training (advanced only) are available.

NEW JERSEY INSTITUTE FOR TRAINING IN PSYCHOANALYSIS

800 Catalpa Avenue
Teaneck, New Jersey 07666
Telephone: 201-836-1065

Year Founded: 1972

Founder(s): Dr. Joel Bernstein and Dr. Neil Wilson

Accredited by: National Association for the Advancement of Psychoanalysis

Affiliated with: None

Psychological Orientation: Classical Psychoanalytic (including subsequent developments in the field)

Duration of Training: 5-year curriculum (additional time for completion of written case presentation)

Current Tuition: $2,190 per year **Supervision Fee:** $20

Registration Fee: $150 per semester

Miscellaneous Fees: Control anaysis fees

Course Fee: $315 per course

Average Class Size: 6-7 **Faculty Members:** 21

Program Admission Requirements:

Candidates must have a master's degree in a mental health field. Prior clinical experience is desirable, but not required. An interview is required.

Program Completion Requirements:

Client Requirements: Not applicable

Personal Analysis: Candidates must undergo a minimum of 470 hours of personal analysis with an analyst graduated from an accredited psychoanalytic institute. Past analysis with an accredited analyst is accepted. Agreement is secured that if there is evidence of need for further work, the candidate will seek additional analysis.

Supervision Requirements: Not applicable

Case Presentation Requirements: There are case presentation courses, with different foci, in each of the 5 years of the program.

Thesis Requirements: A final case presentation is prepared in written form, with the guidance of a specifically formed writing committee. The experience is to be educational as well as evaluative.

Evaluations: Evaluations of each candidate are made yearly to the Training Committee by instructors, supervisors and controls. Only the points of agreement are communicated to the candidate. It is intended that feedback from controls, who are the major source of information to the Training Committee, is to be continuous throughout the ongoing control analysis.

Additional Information:

The New Jersey Institute for Training in Psychoanalysis was founded with the objective of presenting a comprehensive, postgraduate classical Psychoanalytic program for a broad base of interested professionals. The program is thorough and serious, but mild-paced, based on a 5-year evening training curriculum that allows its candidates to learn, think, and do psychoanalysis in an integrated way. Candidates are provided with clinical experience at the Institute's low-cost Psychoanalytic Clinic, Inc., and are helped to become established in the private practice of psychoanalysis.

This program is the first formal Psychoanalytic Training program for nonmedical professionals in the state of New Jersey to be accredited by the National Association for the Advancement of Psychoanalysis, Inc.

INSTITUTE OF SPORTS PSYCHOLOGY

P.O. Box 367
Guadalupita, New Mexico 87722
Telephone: 505-387-2274

Year Founded: 1980s

Founder(s): Kurt A. Krueger and S.G. Somani

Accredited By: Government of India

Affiliated With: Success Systems International

Psychological Orientation: Transpersonal and Humanistic Psychology, Practical Sports Psychology

Duration of Training: 6 to 18 months

Current Tuition: $2,900

Application Fee: $10

Registration Fee: $50

Course Fee: $325 per semester

Seminar Schedule: 14 15-hour classes

Average Class Size: 9

Faculty Members: 9

Annual Applicants: 35

Students Accepted: 15

Enrollment: 30

Graduates: 11

Program Admission Requirements:

Candidates are required to have a B.A. or B.S. in Psychology, Education, or a related field. A minimum of 6 months prior clinical experience is preferred. Candidates must submit a 500-word essay on their goals and objectives for careers in Peak Performance Psychology/Sports Psychology.

Program Completion Requirements:

Seminar Requirements: Candidates must complete 9 of 14 seminars offered.

Client Requirements: Not applicable

Personal Analysis: Candidates must complete 30 hours of transpersonal/Jungian analysis over a two-year period. Past analysis is accepted after a full description is presented.

Supervision Required: Candidates are required to have 20 hours of supervision of 10 control cases over 1 to 2 years.

Case Presentations Required: Candidates are required to give 1 case presentation each month.

Thesis Required: None

Evaluations: Committee evaluations are made based on research papers, case studies, and evaluation seminars/presentations.

Additional Information:

The Institute of Sports Psychology is an educational and research institute training professionals and trainers/coaches for teaching and consulting in Peak Performance Psychology and Practical Sports Psychology. The ISP utilizes a systems approach for full integration of behavioral modification and whole body enhancement for peak performance. This includes: nutrition and fitness exercises and their effects on the body, mind and spirit, intervention techniques for enriching and stabilizing mental and emotional qualities, and spiritual practices to tap the metaphysical abilities inherent in the human form. The Institute prepares a person to be successful as an independent consultant or seminar leader in Peak Performance Psychology for sports, performing arts, business and industry, and the general public. Basic knowledge in setting up an office, marketing, presenting seminar and workshop programs, client communication and follow-up practices is offered along with the psychological seminars and practica.

ADVANCED INSTITUTE FOR ANALYTIC PSYCHOTHERAPY

178-10 Wexford Terrace
Jamaica Estates, New York 11432
Telephone: 718-739-7099/Fax: 718-658-4641

Year Founded: 1958

Founder: Joseph LeBoit

Accredited by: New York State Board of Regents

Affiliated with: Advanced Center for Psychotherapy

Psychological Orientation: Psychoanalytic Psychotherapy and clinical application of the psychologies of Freud, Winnicott, Klein, the British School, and American Ego Psychology

Duration of Training: 4 years on a part-time basis

Current Tuition: $325 per trimester

Application Fee: $25 **Registration Fee:** $25

Course Fee: $150

Seminar Schedule: 24 full-credit courses: 12 lecture, 12 case seminars. Courses cover classic and contemporary theory and technique; resistance, transference, countertransference, narcissism, and dreams form the core curriculum.

Average Class Size: Information not provided

Faculty Members: Information not provided

Program Admission Requirements:

Candidates must be Psychiatrists or Psychologists who have completed or are enrolled in doctoral programs, Social Workers with a master's degree, or Registered Professional Nurses with psychiatric experience.

Program Completion Requirements:

Client Requirements: Clinical practice is arranged by the Institute for the duration of the candidacy.

Personal Analysis: Candidates must undergo a minimum of 350 hours of personal analytic psychotherapy with an analyst selected by the deans. Prior analysis is evaluated.

Supervision Requirements: Candidates must have 180 hours of individual supervision, 50 of which are in continuous case control of 1 case by 1 supervisor.

Case Presentation Requirements: Not applicable

Thesis Requirements: None

Evaluations: Information not provided

BLANTON-PEALE GRADUATE INSTITUTE

3 West 29th Street
New York, New York 10001
Telephone: 212-725-7850/Fax: 212-689-3212

Year Founded: 1937

Founder(s): Norman Vincent Peale and Smiley Blanton, M.D.

Accredited by: American Association of Pastoral Counselors, American Association of Marriage and Family Therapists

Affiliated with: Andover Newton Theological Seminary, New York Theological Seminary, Union Theological Seminary, Fordham University

Psychological Orientation: Psychoanalytic Psychotherapy, Family Systems, Drive Theory, Self Psychology, Ego Psychology, and Object Relations

Duration of Training: 3 years minimum

Current Tuition: $8000 per year plus personal therapy costs

Application Fee: $100 **Registration Fee:** $50

Supervision Fee: $69 **Course Fee:** $220 per course

Seminar Schedule: Tuesday through Thursday from September to June, 17 to 23 courses per year taken over 3 trimesters

Average Class Size: 8 **Faculty Members:** 28

Annual Applicants: 12 **Students Accepted:** 9

Enrollment: 23 **Graduates:** 5

Nonenrolled Students: Professionals may take and audit classes. Audits must be approved by the class instructor and the Director of Training.

Program Admission Requirements:

Candidates must have a master's degree in Theology or in a mental health field. Candidates must have at least 2 years of prior experience or C.P.E. Personal analysis and supervision are required during training with an approved therapist who is not on the Blanton staff or faculty. A screening interview, a faculty committee interview, 2 letters of recommendation, and essays are required.

Program Completion Requirements:

Seminar Requirements: 50 courses

Client Requirements: The Institute provides clients and sponsors treatment, depending on the phase of the candidate's work.

Personal Analysis: Candidates must undergo 2 /week personal psychoanalytic psychotherapy and group or marriage and family therapy for 1400 treatment hours over a 3-to-5-year period. Past analysis is not accepted.

Supervision Requirements: Candidates must receive 450 hours of supervision over a three-year period.

Case Presentation Requirements: One case paper to the entire Institute community is required.

Thesis Requirements: An integrative paper, including a case and theoretical material is required.

Evaluations: Evaluations are conducted every 6 months with a committee of supervisors.

Additional Information:

This is an intense, extensive experience integrating cognitive, clinical, and affective learning. There is also an emphasis on integrating the spiritual journey of the resident into the psychotherapeutic work. The Institute is interfaith, nonsectarian, and nonprofit.

C.G. JUNG INSTITUTE OF NEW YORK

28 East 39th Street
New York, New York 10016
Telephone: 212-986-5458

Year Founded: 1962

Founder(s): Jungian analysts working in the New York area

Accredited by: National Association for the Advancement of Psychoanalysis (NAAP)

Affiliated with: None

Psychological Orientation: Jungian

Duration of Training: 6 years or more, depending on the pace at which the candidate goes through the program

Current Tuition: $1260 per year

Application Fee: $150

Supervision Fee: $12,800 for 4 years

Course Fee: $225 per course per semester

Miscellaneous Fees: $30 annual library fee

Seminar Schedule: Classes are held on Mondays and Tuesdays for 2 semesters each year, 14 weeks each semester.

Average Class Size: 8

Faculty Members: 55

Annual Applicants: 8

Students Accepted: 3

Enrollment: 2

Graduates: 3

Nonenrolled Students: Members of the Professional Society of Jungian Analysts may audit or take classes. Candidates from other Jungian training programs may also take or audit classes.

Program Admission Requirements: Candidates must have a master's degree in a mental health field or an acceptable equivalent. Candidates must have had 50 hours of supervised clinical work. Candidates must be licensed to practice in the state where they are working. Candidates must have 150 hours of Jungian analysis and 50 hours of supervision. An application form, academic transcripts, an autobiography, 3 essays, letters from a supervisor, 1 pre-admission interview to precede the formal application, and 1 or 2 admissions interviews with the Admissions Committee are required.

Program Completion Requirements:

Seminar Requirements: Candidates are required to complete 2 credits of course work and 12 credits of case seminars (6 full years).

Client Requirements: Candidates are required to see a minimum of 10 clients per week for 5 years. The fee is to be determined by the candidate and the analysand. The C.G. Jung Referral Service refers analysands seeking Jungian analysis at low fees to the candidates.

Personal Analysis: Candidates are required to complete at least 400 hours of personal analysis in sessions occurring at least once per week throughout training; twice per week is recommended. The analyst must be a member of the Professional Society of Jungian Analysts. Candidates must have a minimum of 150 hours of analysis prior to admission.

Supervision Requirements: A total of 400 hours of supervision are required over 6 years, including 2 control cases: 1) For referral service analysands, 160 hours of supervision are required over 4 years; 2) For private practice, weekly supervision of 160 hours over 4 years is required; and 3) Control cases must be supervised for at least 80 hours over 2 years.

Case Presentation Requirements: One case presentation is required each semester for a total minimum of 12 presentations.

Thesis Requirements: A paper of publishable quality on an aspect of Jungian practice done during 5th and 6th year is required for graduation.

Evaluations: Each candidate's work is reviewed annually by the Evaluation Committee. After the completion of 3 years, an interview with the Evaluation Committee is required before promotion to the advanced stage of training. An interview with the Evaluation Committee can be requested by supervisor, faculty, or candidate if problems arise.

Additional Information:

The C.G. Jung Institute of New York is a post graduatuate training program in Jungian analysis. It aims to develop clinical competence in mature individuals with a sustained interest in the psychology of people who have a readiness to develop and maintain a fruitful relationship with the unconscious and its symbolic expression. Candidates are required to be in Jungian analysis throughout training.

Courses are in 3 areas: 1) Jungian Theory; 2) Clinical applications of Jungian theory and case seminars; and 3) Archetypal symbolism--the study of symbolic expression through which human beings understand their world--mythologies of various cultures, folk tales, and other manifestations of the collective unconscious.

Individual supervision in clinical work is required throughout training. The Institute is located in the C.G. Jung Center, which also houses the C.G. Jung Foundation, the sponsor of public programs and the publisher of the journal Quadrant, a book store, a library with more than 10,000 volumes, and tapes on Jungian and other schools of depth psychology, and the Archive for Research in Archetypal Symbolism (ARAS), which is devoted to the study of symbolic imagery with 13,000 images of cultural importance.

CENTER FOR FAMILY LEARNING

28 Rye Brook Plaza
Rye Brook, New York 10573
Telephone: 914-253-9190

Year Founded: 1973

Founder(s): Phillip J. Guerin Jr., M.D. and Thomas Fogarty, M.D.

Accredited by: New York State Board of Regents

Affiliated with: None

Psychological Orientation: Bowenian family systems theory and therapy

Duration of Training: 1 to 3 years for externships of fellowships

Current Tuition: $2,500 per year

Application Fee: $50

Seminar Schedule: 30 hours per year for 4 years (120 seminar hours)

Average Class Size: 9 **Faculty Members:** 10

Annual Applicants: 25 **Students Accepted:** 6

Enrollment: 6 **Graduates:** 12

Nonenrolled Students: The Institute allows both professionals and continuing education nonprofessionals to take occasional classes. Under an arrangement with the Director, a one-time audit is permitted.

Program Admission Requirements:

Candidates must have an M.A. or its equivalent in Psychology, Social Work, Education, Counseling, Guidance, or Ministry. Candidates must have 2 years of clinical experience with a wide variety of families. Candidates must have a 1-hour personal interview conducted by the Director of Education and faculty members.

Program Completion Requirements:

Seminar Requirements: Candidates must participate and present in 5 hours of seminar work each week.

Client Requirements: Not applicable

Personal Analysis: Candidates should have completed 2 to 3 years of individual psychoanalytic, family, or marital therapy.

Supervision Requirements: Candidates receive an hour of supervision per week, using videotaped client sessions for the entire program: 5 control cases are studied, as well as the candidates' own families.

Case Presentation Requirements: Candidates are required to present every week for an hour.

Thesis Requirements: None

Evaluations: Candidates are evaluated twice per year in January and June. Supervisors and faculty are also evaluated by the candidates.

Additional Information:

The Center for Family Learning is a nonprofit educational institute with offices in New Rochelle and Rye Brook. It is recognized throughout the country and overseas for its postgraduate education of professionals, innovative community educational programs, and professional publications and clinical research into family psychiatry. The Center supports an ongoing treatment service and clinical research projects in the study of current problems faced by individuals and families.

The Center believes that emotional, physical, psychological, and behavioral problems experienced by an individual and/or relationship problems between family members are best treated within the context of the family. Therapy ranges from short term symptom relief to long-term quality of life perspective, while respecting individual financial constraints.

CENTER FOR MODERN PSYCHOANALYTIC STUDIES

16 West 10th Street
New York, New York 10011
Telephone: 212-260-7050/Fax: 212-260-7052

Year Founded: 1971

Founder(s): Evelyn Abrams, Dorothy Bloch, Selwyn Brody, Ethel Goldwater Clevans, Mark Clevans, Irene Kesten, Jacob Kesten, William Kerman,

Evelyn Liegner, Leonard Leigner, Shirley B. Love, Sydney I. Love, Benjamin D. Margolis, Deborah Margolis, Cyril Z. Meadow, Phyllis W. Meadow, Benjamin Nelson, Marie Coleman Nelson, Joan Ormond, Louis Ormond, Leslie Rosenthal, and Harold Stern

Accredited by: No accreditation

Affiliated with: None

Psychological Orientation: Modern Freudian

Duration of Training: A minimum of 4 years

Current Tuition: $1000 annually

Application Fee: $35 **Registration Fee:** $40

Supervision Fee: Arranged individually, early supervision $275 per semester

Miscellaneous Fees: Referral service - $425/semester

Course Fee: $200 per course

Seminar Schedule: 1 1/2 hours per week for 15 weeks (afternoon and evening classes)

Average Class Size: 15 **Faculty Members:** 40+

Annual Applicants: 40 **Students Accepted:** 30

Enrollment: 28 **Graduates:** 17

Program Admission Requirements:

Candidates must have an undergraduate degree to be interviewed for admission, but they must have a master's degree for certificate candidacy. No prior clinical experience is required. Candidates must submit an application form, an optional essay, and undergo an interview. Analytic experience is required.

Program Completion Requirements:

Seminar Requirements: Candidates must complete 8 courses in theory, 8 clinical courses, 8 field courses, 8 maturation courses, and 4 history courses.

Client Requirements: Candidates must work with 3 cases simultaneously for an extended period. Fees are determined by the candidate and the patient.

Personal Analysis: Candidates must undergo 450 sessions of personal analysis with a Modern Analyst, 150 hours of which may be in a group.

Supervision Requirements: Candidates must have 50 hours of supervision of 1 to 2 cases with 3 different supervisors.

Case Presentation Requirements: Case presentations are made frequently.

Thesis Requirements: A final research project is required.

Evaluations: Candidates must meet requirements. Candidates may request an educational advisement interview at any time. Advisement is required at various stages.

Additional Information:

The curricula and reading lists established by The Center for Modern Analysis are followed by institutes throughout the United States. The Center is frequently called upon to aid other institutions in setting a curriculum. The Center Publishes *Modern Psychoanalysis,* which is distributed nationally and internationally.

CENTER FOR REICHIAN ENERGETIC THERAPY

310 West 86th Street
New York, New York 10024
Telephone: 212-580-9096

Year Founded: 1986

Founder(s): Bernard Rosenblum, M.D.

Accredited by: No accreditation

Affiliated with: None

Psychological Orientation: Reichian

Duration of Training: 3 years

Current Tuition: $1200 per year

Seminar Schedule: Friday night and all day Saturday, every third weekend from September through June.

Average Class Size: 7

Faculty Members: 1

Annual Applicants: 12

Students Accepted: 8

Enrollment: 7

Graduates: 5

Program Admission Requirements:

Candidates must hold a graduate degree in a mental health field (some exceptions are made). Candidates require a personal interview.

Program Completion Requirements:

Client Requirements: It is suggested that candidates see clients by the third year.

Personal Analysis: Reichean Bioenergetic or Core Energetic therapy is recommended. Past therapy is accepted.

Supervision Requirements: Supervision of 3 to 5 control cases over 3 years is required.

Case Presentation Requirements: Candidates give several case presentations.

Thesis Requirements: None

Evaluations: The candidate is evaluated for his/her theoretical understanding, mastery of therapeutic technique, and emotional sensitivity.

Additional Information:

The Center for Reichean Energetic Therapy is a humanistically oriented learning program based on the Body-Mind Therapy developed by Wilhelm Reich. Other orientations are also studied, including Bioenergetics, Gestalt, and Reichean techniques of working with the body and character armor and release of depth emotion and energy, in conjunction with a sensitive understanding of the therapist-patient relationship. The connection between current functioning and childhood is thoroughly developed, and effective use of fantasy, imagination, and role playing are taught. Students also learn to relate in a direct, emotional, and intimate way with each other.

CENTER FOR THE ADVANCEMENT OF GROUP STUDIES

250 W. 57th Street Suite 1527
New York, New York 10107
Telephone: 212-721-8642/Fax: 718-631-5971

Year Founded: 1988

Founder(s): Louis R. Ormont, Ph.D.

Accredited by: No accreditation

Affiliated with: None

Psychological Orientation: Modern Group Process, Louis R. Ormont, Hyman Spotnitz, Azya Kadis, Fritz Perls, Theodore Reik, D.W. Winnicott, Alexander Wolf, and the National Training Laboratories

Duration of Training: Students may complete requirements at their own pace; however, students are encouraged to complete the program within 8 years.

Current Tuition: $250 per course

Application Fee: $25

Supervision Fee: $250

Course Fee: $250 per course

Seminar Schedule: 12 1 1/2-hour courses per semester

Average Class Size: 8

Faculty Members: 57

Annual Applicants: 57

Students Accepted: 57

Enrollment: 110

Graduates: 0

Nonenrolled Students: Professionals and nonprofessionals may take or audit occasional classes in the Center's lecture series.

Program Admission Requirements:

Candidates must be licensed or certified Psychiatrists, Psychologists, Social Workers, Psychiatric Nurses, Pastoral Counselors, or students in these fields. Candidates must display evidence of personal aptitude and life experience. Licencing and certification are required for the Therapeutic Track only. A personal interview is required for admission.

Program Completion Requirements:

Seminar Requirements: Candidates must complete 20 courses for each track, 12 of which are basic courses. Students must take at least 1 course within any 3-year-period to be considered an active participant in the program.

Client Requirements: During the second year of study, students on the Therapeutic Track co-lead a group with an experienced professional who serves as an informal mentor. In the third year, students conduct their own group. Communications Track students conduct a field work group in an agency affiliated with the Outreach Program or in an institution that offers an opportunity to obtain this experience. Therapeutic and Communications Track students conduct different types of groups. The former conduct groups focusing on pathology; the latter lead groups stressing personal and interpersonal enrichment, emotional growth, preventive mental hygiene, social action or supervision.

Personal Analysis: Candidates must complete 150 hours of group analysis, and 100 sessions of concurrent individual treatment.

Supervision Requirements: Candidates must complete 75 sessions of group supervision, and 30 sessions of individual supervision.

Case Presentation Requirements: Candidates must present a final paper that advances theoretical, technical, practical, or clinical knowledge in the field of modern group process.

Thesis Requirements: None

Evaluations: Ongoing semester evaluations of course work and supervision are conducted. The Center requires verification of hours of group and individual analysis, submission of field work completion form, evidence of completion of case presentations, ongoing evaluation by supervisors, acceptance of a final paper, and presentation to faculty of a group process.

Additional Information:

The Center's training programs prepare graduates to provide people in groups with the emotional education they need to overcome hampering patterns and to immunize them against their return. Training is holistic and involves course work, supervised field work, and personal growth experiences in individual and group settings. Students are taught to conduct groups of all types and sizes in a variety of settings. They learn to decipher interpersonal patterns and to develop constructive interchanges among group members. The Center emphasizes the use of emotional reactions to understand and to influence nonconstructive behavior.

FAMILY INSTITUTE OF WESTCHESTER

147 Archer Avenue
Mount Vernon, New York 10550
Telephone: 914-699-4300

Year Founded: 1977

Founder(s): Betty Carter, Eloise Julius, Fredda Herz, Kenneth Terkelsen, Norman Ackerman, David Berenson, and Monica McGoldrick

Accredited by: New York State Board of Regents

Affiliated with: None

Psychological Orientation: Family Therapy

Duration of Training: 3 to 5 years

Current Tuition: $2200 to $2800 per year

Course Fee: $75 for 1-day courses; $450 for Introductory Theory

Seminar Schedule: Supervision groups—9 or 10 groups, 3-5 hours per week

Average Class Size: 12

Faculty Members: 13

Enrollment: 64

Graduates: 12

Nonenrolled Students: Professionals may take only the 1-day courses offered by the Institute.

Program Admission Requirements:

Candidates must have a graduate degree in Social Work, Psychology, Medicine, or Psychiatric Nursing. Other mental health professionals, including clergy, may take the Introductory Theory Seminar. Candidates must have 2 years of clinical experience in seeing families. A personal interview, curriculum vitae, and letters of recommendation are required. Occasionally a videotape of a family session may be requested.

Program Completion Requirements:

Seminar Requirements: Candidates must complete 3 years in the Intensive Program and 2 years in the Externship Program.

Client Requirements: Candidates must complete 3 to 5 client sessions per week. Only Externs see clients in the FIW clinic.

Personal Analysis: Not applicable

Supervision Requirements: Candidates must complete 120 to 130 hours of supervision over 2 to 3 years.

Case Presentation Requirements: Case presentations are given every 3 or 4 weeks.

Thesis Requirements: None

Evaluations: Self-evaluations are required 3 times a year. Supervisors give regular evaluations, both written and oral. No letter grades are given.

Additional Information:

The Family Institute of Westchester integrates concepts common to a variety of family systems models, including structural, Bowenian, and strategic. The Institute focuses on the process of therapy rather than a particular "brand" of Family Therapy. Thus, training focuses on: 1) engagement; 2) assessment and treatment planning; 3) treatment implementation; and 4) termination and/or referral. These objectives are addressed in different ways in both the theory courses and the supervision process. For instance, in the first theory course, trainees learn about engagement and asssessment with an emphasis on developing a broader lens for doing evaluation and treatment planning. In supervision, faculty focus on helping trainees conduct an interview from which relevant information can be obtained for formulating a hypothesis about the family's problem. In the second year of the program, there is a greater refinement of the trainees' skills in this area, such as developing a standard yet flexible way of collecting initial information from families and using the information to make meaningful interventions.

In learning about treatment implementation, trainees are taught increasingly complex and varied models of intervention. In supervision, faculty assist trainees in finding interventions appropriate to the trainee's personal style and to the family's problem, ethnicity, and resistance. Generally, the Institute has found that trainees initially feel most comfortable with structural interventions, later developing proficiency in working with strategic and Bowenian approaches.

Trainees are taught to approach treatment with an investigative approach to each clinical decision—leading to some further options and cutting off the path to others. They're taught to think through their interventions and the rationale for them.

GESTALT CENTER OF LONG ISLAND

57 Bounty Lane
Jericho, New York 11753
Telephone: 516-931-5383

Year Founded: 1977

Founder(s): Jerome Gold, Ed.D. and Kenneth Meyer, Ph.D.

Accredited by: New York State Board of Regents, Provisional Charter

Affiliated with: None

Psychological Orientation: Gestalt Psychotherapy

Duration of Training: 3-level training program usually taking between 3 and 4 years

Current Tuition: $2000 per year

Application Fee: $25

Supervision Fee: $70 per month for 8 months for third-level supervision.

Miscellaneous Fees: $120 room and board for 2 weekends per year

Seminar Schedule: Five 7-hour courses per year, and 1 weekly training group for 2 1/2 hours from October to May.

Average Class Size: 15

Faculty Members: 20

Annual Applicants: 12

Students Accepted: 10

Enrollment: 40

Graduates: 5

Nonenrolled Students: Professionals are permitted to attend the weekend intensives. The Institute also sponsors annual conferences that are open to the public.

Program Admission Requirements:

Candidates must have a master's degree in a behavioral science in order to attend the program. Prior clinical experience is preferred, but not required. Candidates must be eligible for licensure by the State of New York in order to be certified and receive a certificate. Candidates must submit letters of recommendation and have a personal interview.

Program Completion Requirements:

Seminar Requirements: Candidates are required to complete approximately 100 hours of course work (5 courses each year).

Client Requirements: Not applicable

Personal Analysis: Candidates must complete 90 hours of personal therapy with a Gestalt Therapist, approved by the Center. A year of prior therapy may be approved.

Supervision Requirements: Candidates receive a minimum of 32 hours of supervision over a 1-year period. In addition, there is a supervised training group at each level.

Case Presentation Requirements: Not applicable

Thesis Requirements: A formal colloquium presentation is required before graduation.

Evaluations: Detailed evaluations of a candidate's performance are made after each trimester of the second- and third-level training group.

Additional Information:

The Gestalt Center of Long Island offers a certificate program of postgraduate training in Gestalt Psychotherapy. It offers a shorter 1-year professional training program, an annual day-long conference on Gestalt methods, film showings, lectures, demonstrations and intensive training weekends. The Center's faculty have postgraduate training in Gestalt psychotherapy and extensive experience in institutional and private practice settings.

The Center's 3-level training program provides a didactic and experiential base for acquiring the theoretical underpinnings and technical skills of Gestalt Psychotherapy. Courses include: Experiential Psychotherapy—Theory and Practice, Developmental Psychology, Psychology of the Body and Body Work, Psychodynamics, Theory of Neurosis, Treatment of Neurosis, Ethics, and Case Seminar.

GESTALT THERAPY CENTER OF QUEENS

33-54 164th Street
Flushing, New York 11358
Telephone: 718 461-9022

Year Founded: 1984

Founder(s): Norman Friedman and Michael Spindell

Accredited by: Information not provided

Affiliated with: Gestalt Center of Long Island, Gestalt Center for Psychotherapy and Training NYC, Gestalt Associates for Psychotherapy, NYC

Psychological Orientation: Gestalt Therapy and Clinical Social Work

Duration of Training: Varies depending on the needs of the trainee

Current Tuition: $50 per 2-hour session in group

Supervision Fee: $60

Seminar Schedule: 2 hours every other week through the academic year

Average Class Size: 4

Faculty Members: 2

Annual Applicants: 5

Students Accepted: 4

Enrollment: 3

Nonenrolled Students: Both professionals and nonprofessionals are permitted to take classes.

Program Admission Requirements:

Candidates normally are required to have a relevant graduate degree, but this is flexible in relation to the person's interests, skills, and potentials. Some clinical experience is preferred. Certification/licensing is preferred. Personal therapy is recommended for admission. Personal interviews are required for admission.

Program Completion Requirements:

Seminar Requirements: Completion occurs when a candidate feels her/his needs have been met.

Client Requirements: Not applicable

Personal Analysis: Not applicable

Supervision Requirements: Supervision is recommended, though not required.

Case Presentation Requirements: Case presentations are made as needed.

Thesis Requirements: None

Evaluations: Time is set aside for personal interviews once or twice a year, during which faculty evaluate the trainee and the trainee evaluates the faculty.

Additional Information:

The training program emphasizes Gestalt philosophy, which is the avoidance of arbitrary power structures in favor of emerging figures. The approach is process oriented.

GREENWICH INSTITUTE FOR PSYCHOANALYTIC STUDIES

10 West 10th Street
New York, New York 10011
Telephone: 212-989-2990

Year Founded: 1962

Accredited by: New York State Department of Education

Affiliated with: Fifth Avenue Center for Counseling and Psychotherapy

Psychological Orientation: Eclectic, Ego Pscyhology, Self Psychology, Object Relations, Drive Therapy, Intersubjective and Relational Models

Duration of Training: 3-year program

Current Tuition: $560 per year

Seminar Schedule: Fridays, 4 classes 9:00 A.M. to 1:30 P.M.

Average Class Size: 12 **Faculty Members:** 24

Enrollment: 32

Nonenrolled Students: The Institute occasionally allows professionals and nonprofessionals to take or audit classes;, each case is evaluated on a personal basis.

Program Admission Requirements:

Candidates must have an M.S.W., 60 credits towards a Ph.D. in Psychology, or a master's degree in Nursing. Prior clinical experience is not necessary. Social Work certification is preferred. Candidates must have interviews with 2 senior members of the Institute.

Program Completion Requirements:

Seminar Requirements: Candidates must attend 12 seminars (26 to 30 sessions each) plus 12 minicourses (5 sessions each).

Client Requirements: Candidates must conduct 950 client sessions during the 3-year period. A per-patient fee is paid to the candidate.

Personal Analysis: Candidates must have at least 300 hours of psychoanalytically oriented psychotherapy. Past analysis is accepted.

Supervision Requirements: Candidates receive 150 hours of supervision during the 3-year period.

Case Presentation Requirements: Case presentations are given routinely as part of case seminar courses. Each student must formally present a case as a requirement for graduation.

Thesis Requirements: None

Evaluations: Primary evaluations are provided by the supervisors. Additional evaluations are provided to the supervisor by the instructors of each seminar.

HUNTINGTON THERAPY INSTITUTE

2 Murray Court
Huntington, New York 11743
Telephone: 516-673-1293

Year Founded: 1987

Founder(s): Bonney Gulino-Schaub, M.S., R.N., C.S., and Richard Schaub, Ph.D.

Accredited by: Private association

Affiliated with: Psychosynthesis Institute of New York

Psychological Orientation: Transpersonal

Duration of Training: 3 years **Current Tuition:** $1200 per year

Supervision Fee: Varies

Miscellaneous Fees: Summer training retreat

Seminar Schedule: 1 Saturday per month from September to June.

Average Class Size: 12 **Faculty Members:** 4

Annual Applicants: 25 **Students Accepted:** 14

Enrollment: 14 **Graduates:** 11

Nonenrolled Students: Professionals may take occasional classes; nonprofesionals may take self-development classes.

Program Admission Requirements:

Candidates must hold a graduate degree in a recognized helping profession. Candidates must have 1 year of prior clinical experience. A personal interview is required.

Program Completion Requirements:

Client Requirements: Not applicable

Personal Analysis: Candidates must have an in-depth therapeutic relationship. The number of hours, years, and type of analysis may vary. Past analysis is accepted.

Supervision Requirements: The number of hours and control cases in supervision, as well as the duration, depend on the candidate's clinical experience.

Case Presentation Requirements: Case presentations depend on the candidate's clinical experience.

Thesis Requirements: None

Evaluations: Evaluations are given at mid-year and end-year mentoring meetings.

Additional Information:

The Institute is a training and research association for psychosynthesis and Transpersonal Psychology. The institute integrates the theories and techniques that include the biological, psychological, social, and spiritual realities of both the client and the helping professional. As such, the Institute offers a clear alternative to pathology-oriented therapies. In addition to learning a comprehensive and practical model of depth psychotherapy, trainees receive extensive training in clinical imagery, clinical meditation, and Hypnotherapy. With these skills, the trainees bring new depth to their agency work and private practices.

Many trainees have received continuing education credits, employer reimbursement, and/or external doctoral credit for Institute study. Classes are held in Manhattan and Huntington (1 hour by train or car from Manhattan).

INSTITUTE FOR CLINICAL HYPNOSIS

619 Middle Neck Road
Great Neck, New York 11023
Telephone: 212-947-3270

Year Founded: 1989

Founder(s): Martin Sabba, Ph.D.

Accredited by: No accreditation **Affiliated with:** None

Psychological Orientation: Hypnotherapy

Duration of Training: 30 hours

Current Tuition: $695

Seminar Schedule: 3 days and seminar attendance

Average Class Size: 6-9

Faculty Members: 2

Annual Applicants: 20

Students Accepted: 6

Enrollment: 6

Graduates: 6

Program Admission Requirements:

The program is open to mental health professionals with graduate degrees, graduate students in mental health, and those wishing to enter the field.

Program Completion Requirements:

Client Requirements: Not applicable

Personal Analysis: Not applicable

Supervision Requirements: Not applicable

Case Presentation Requirements: Not applicable

Thesis Requirements: None

Evaluations: Information not provided

INSTITUTE FOR CONTEMPORARY PSYCHOTHERAPY

1 West 91st Street
New York, New York 10024
Telephone: 212-595-3444

Year Founded: 1971

Founder(s): Fred Lipschitz, Ph.D., William O'Donnell, Ph.D., Irving Schwartz, Ph.D., and Mildred Schwartz, Ph.D.

Accredited by: New York State Board of Regents

Affiliated with: None

Psychological Orientation: Interpersonal/Eclectic

Duration of Training: 4 to 5 years

Current Tuition: $1000 per year

Application Fee: $50 **Supervision Fee:** $30

Miscellaneous Fees: $25-$50 per trimester for materials

Seminar Schedule: Three 1 1/2-hour classes each trimester, for Three 10-week trimesters per year. Classes are held on Wednesdays from 12:00 P.M. to 5:30 P.M.

Average Class Size: 11 **Faculty Members:** 30

Annual Applicants: 15 **Enrollment:** 40

Graduates: 144

Program Admission Requirements:

Candidates must have a Ph.D., M.S.W., or R.N. Prior clinical experience varies according to the individual. Two personal interviews and 3 letters of recommendation are required.

Program Completion Requirements:

Seminar Requirements: 36 seminars

Client Requirements: Candidates must complete 1200 patient hours, including 420 hours of 3-times-a-week psychoanalysis, in order to graduate. Candidates are paid $6 to $10 per hour, depending upon the number of hours accrued. Private referrals are given, based upon the number of hours accrued.

Personal Analysis: Candidates must complete 400 hours of personal analysis during a 4-year period with a graduate of a recognized analytic training program. Past analysis is not accepted.

Supervision Requirements: Candidates must receive 320 hours of supervision during a 4-year period and must have 2 control cases.

Case Presentation Requirements: One case presentation is required in the third year.

Thesis Requirements: None

Evaluations: Evaluations are required once per year by 1 supervisor during the first year, and by 2 supervisors each following year. Supervisors meet with the Training Committee. More frequent evaluations are done if required.

Additional Information:

The aims of the Institute for Contemporary Psychotherapy are to provide training in Psychoanalysis and Psychoanalytic Psychotherapy for qualified professionals and to provide, at moderate cost, a full range of psychotherapeutic services.

ICP's philosophy is that the development of treatment skills and competence can best be carried out in a setting in which the continued personal growth of the therapist is fostered. The program, therefore, emphasizes the development of technical skill and theoretical knowledge. The clinical services of the Institute provide Psychoanalysis and Psychoanalytic Psychotherapy for a current population of more than 500 patients per week. The Center for the Study of Anorexia and Bulimia is a division of I.C.P.

INSTITUTE FOR EXPRESSIVE ANALYSIS

325 West End Avenue, Suite 12B
New York, New York 10023
Telephone: 212-362-5085

Year Founded: 1981

Founder(s): Arthur Robbins

Accredited by: National Association for the Advancement of Psychoanalysis (NAAP)

Affiliated with: None

Psychological Orientation: Psychoanalytic Psychotherapy, Object Relations, Self Psychology, Jungian Analysis, Traditional Psychoanalysis

Duration of Training: 3 to 4 years

Current Tuition: $125 per 8-week course

Application Fee: $25 **Registration Fee:** $25

Average Class Size: Information not provided

Faculty Members: 20 **Annual Applications:** 10

Program Admission Requirements:

Candidates are required to have a master's degree in the Social Sciences. Candidates must have 1 year of clinical experience. Candidates are required to have 100 hours of personal treatment for admission. A personal interview and a letter of recommendation are required for admission.

Program Completion Requirements:

Seminar Requirements: Candidates are required to complete 32 courses.

Client Requirements: Candidates are required to conduct 400 supervised client sessions, including 100 hours with each of 2 patients.

Personal Analysis: Candidates must have 400 hours of personal therapy or analysis with a Psychoanalytic Psychotherapist. Past analysis with an analyst acceptable to the Institute is accepted.

Supervision Requirements: Candidates must have 120 hours of supervision over a 2-year period including 2 control cases.

Case Presentation Requirements: Not applicable

*Thesis Requirement*s: None

Evaluations: Evaluations are given by instructors and supervisors.

Additional Information:

The Institute for Expressive Analysis is dedicated to an ongoing dialogue concerning creative currents in contemporary psychoanalytic thinking. It aims to build a solid clinical background useful for both institutional work and private practice, with an emphasis on artistry in therapy along with a scientific understanding of developmental issues. The fundamentals of clinical work are combined with an integration of what is best in a variety of verbal and nonverbal approaches.

INSTITUTE FOR INTEGRATIVE PSYCHOTHERAPY

500 East 85th Street
New York, New York 10028
Telephone: 212-734-5291/Fax: 212-879-6618

Year Founded: 1972

Founder(s): Richard G. Erskine, Ph.D.

Accredited by: No accreditation

Affiliated with: International Transactional Analysis Association (ITAA), American Group Psychotherapy Association (AGPA), New York Institute for Gestalt Therapy, Society for the Exploration of Psychotherapy Integration (SEPI), New York Joint Council for Mental Health Services.

Psychological Orientation: Integrative Psychotherapy: Affective, Behavioral, Cognitive (primary), Transactional Analysis, Object Relations, Self Psychology, Existential.

Duration of Training: 4 years average

Current Tuition: $2250.00

Supervision Fee: $60 per hour

Miscellaneous Fees: $1700 for 10-day workshop

Seminar Schedule: Meets 5 times a year for 3 days

Average Class Size: 16 **Faculty Members:** 2

Annual Applicants: 75 **Students Accepted:** 71

Enrollment: 71

Nonenrolled Students: Professionals can participate in the 10-day intensive training workshop. No reading is required for the summer intensive.

Program Admission Requirements:

Candidates must be mental health professionals working within the field. Prior clinical experience is not necessary. The program will accept graduate students. Prior certification or licensing is not necessary, but a personal interview is required.

Program Completion Requirements:

Client Requirements: No client work is required.

Personal Analysis: The number of hours and years of personal analysis

Personal Analysis: The number of hours and years of personal analysis varies with each individual. No specific type of analyst is required. Past analysis is acceptable.

Supervision Requirements: Approximately 150 hours of supervision.

Case Presentation Requirements: 1 every 2 months after the first year

Thesis Requirements: None.

Evaluations: Evaluation consists of a case presentation with audiotapes and a demonstrated capacity to apply theory to clinical practice, to show empathy, clinical acumen, and treatment planning.

Additional Information:

Participants meet for a 3-day weekend 5 times a year in a retreat setting. Each meeting consists of a didactic/theory presentation with a possible demonstration, case consultation and supervision, and group process sessions.

INSTITUTE FOR MODERN PSYCHOANALYSIS

112 West 87th Street
New York, New York 10024
Telephone: 212-496-9043

Year Founded: 1979

Founder(s): Dr. Gerald Lucas and Dr. Marie Lucas

Accredited by: Provisional Charter from the New York State Board of Regents. Accredited by the National Association for the Advancement of Psychoanalysis.

Affiliated with: None

Psychological Orientation: IMP embraces in its curriculum all of the major psychoanalytic traditions including classical Psychoanalysis, Object Relations, Ego and Self Psychology Schools.

Duration of Training: 2 certificate programs—Psychoanalytic Psychotherapy, (3 years) and Psychoanalysis (4 years).

Current Tuition: Per course

Application Fee: $30 **Registration Fee:** $25

Supervision Fee: Group - $275, individual supervision fee by arrangement with the supervisor. (Additional $30 postdated check fee for 3-installment payment plan)

Miscellaneous Fees: $15 late registration fee

Course Fee: $185 per course

Seminar Schedule: The majority of classes are held on Saturdays from 8:30 A.M. to 2:30 P.M. There are some mid-week evening courses. Most courses are 1 1/2 hours long.

Average Class Size: Information not provided

Faculty Members: Information not provided

Program Admission Requirements:

Candidates must have a licensable master's degree in a mental health field in order to matriculate. Prior clinical experience is not a requirement. Candidates must submit a completed application form and have a personal interview.

Program Completion Requirements:

Seminar Requirements: For the Psychoanalytic Pychotherapy program, candidates must complete 24 courses and 6 group supervisions, and for the Psychoanalysis Program, 32 courses and 6 group supervisions (all are 1 semester each).

Client Requirements: Candidates must complete 300 hours of approved, supervised clinical experience before beginning control cases. Previous experience is accepted.

Personal Analysis: Candidates in the Psychoanalytic Psychotherapy program must receive 250 hours of personal analysis throughout their training with an NAAP registered analyst. For Psychoanalytic candidates, the number of hours is 300. Past analysis is accepted.

Supervision Requirements: Candidates in the Psychoanalytic Psychottherapy program receive 50 hours of individual supervision and see 2 control cases for 2 years. Psychoanalytic candidates receive 100 hours of individual supervision and see 3 control cases for 2 years.

Case Presentation Requirements: All candidates present cases in 4 case presentation courses, as well as a final case presentation.

Thesis Requirements: Paper is required.

Evaluations: Instructors complete written evaluations on each student for every course.

Additional Information:

The Institute for Modern Psychoanalysis is a small school with a personal atmosphere. Its specialized instruction provides the student with the opportunity to expand his or her knowledge base and to develop a strong working knowledge of the field of psychoanalysis, and to become adept at the unique techniques and principles that underlie Modern Psychoanalysis.

INSTITUTE FOR PSYCHOANALYTIC TRAINING AND RESEARCH

1651 Third Avenue, Suite 201
New York, New York 10128
Telephone: 212-427-7070

Year Founded: 1958

Founder(s): Lillian Gordon, May Fine Lipson, Elizabeth McNeill, Edward Frankel, Abram Levine, Edward Weill, Erwin Herbst, and Ruth Wolfson

Accredited by: New York State Board of Regents

Affiliated with: International Psychoanalytical Association

Psychological Orientation: Contemporary Freudian Perspective

Duration of Training: 4 years of course work plus 2 control cases

Current Tuition: 1,025 per year

Application Fee: $25 **Registration Fee:** $25

Supervision Fee: Arranged with supervisor

Miscellaneous Fees: Personal analysis 4 times per week

Course Fee: $125 per 8-week course

Seminar Schedule: Eight 8-week courses; courses are 1 1/2 hours long and are given on Monday and Wednesday evenings.

Average Class Size: 5-6

Faculty Members: 27

Annual Applicants: 10

Students Accepted: 7

Enrollment: 63

Graduates: 4

Program Admission Requirements:

Candidates must have a master's degree or are currently are earning one. Prior clinical experience is desirable. Both licensed and non-licesed applicants are accepted. Two interviews, 2 letters of recommendation, and graduate school transcripts are required for admission.

Program Completion Requirements:

Seminar Requirements: Candidates are required to take 27 seminars.

Client Requirements: Candidates see 2 clients 4 times per week. Payment is arranged between analyst and patient. Candidates from outside the traditional fields are required to have a minimum of 6 client hours per week prior to readiness for control.

Personal Analysis: Personal analysis is required 4 times weekly with an IPTAR Training Analyst. The duration is determined by analyst and analysand. Past analysis with an IPTAR Training Analyst is accepted, though candidates may need another analysis during control work.

Supervision Requirements: Weekly supervision is provided for 2 control cases; 1 case for 3 years and 1 case for 2 years.

Case Presentation Requirements: One case presentation is required.

Thesis Requirements: None

Evaluations: A matriculation interview is held at the end of the first year of classes; written and oral Readiness for Control Examinations are taken at the end of the second year of classes; a final case presentation is made after 3 years of control supervision, and an interview is held prior to graduation.

INSTITUTE FOR RATIONAL-EMOTIVE THERAPY

45 East 65th Street
New York, New York 10021
Telephone: 212-535-0822/Fax: 212-249-3582

Year Founded: 1968

Founder(s): Albert Ellis, Ph.D.

Accredited by: New York State Board of Regents

Affiliated with: None

Psychological Orientation: Cognitive-Behavioral

Duration of Training: Fellowship training is 2 years; Internship is 1 year.

Current Tuition: $5000 per year

Seminar Schedule: 16 hours per week

Average Class Size: 9

Faculty Members: Information not provided

Annual Applicants: 40

Students Accepted: 10

Enrollment: 8

Graduates: 8

Nonenrolled Students: Professionals and nonprofessionals may take or audit classes within the professionals Primary Certificate Training Program or the Visiting Professional Program.

Program Admission Requirements:

Candidates must have an M.S.W., Ph.D., or Ed.D. in Counseling Psychology. Predoctoral or postdoctoral clinical experience is required. Candidates must be licensed or eligible. References for a license, 2 personal interviews, and an essay are required.

Program Completion Requirements:

Seminar Requirements: There is a weekly, hour-long clinical seminar.

Client Requirements: Candidates must see 9 clients per week and co-lead a weekly group. $35 per individual client will be paid directly to the Institute.

Personal Analysis: Not applicable

Supervision Requirements: Candidates must receive 3 1/2 hours of supervision at the Institute for Rational-Emotive Therapy over a 2-year period for the Fellowship, and over a 1-year period for the internship.

Case Presentation Requirements: Not applicable

Thesis Requirements: None

Evaluations: Information not provided

INSTITUTE OF CORE ENERGETICS

115 East 23rd Street
New York, New York 10010
Telephone: 212-505-6767

Year Founded: 1983

Founder(s): John C. Peirrakos, M.D.

Accredited by: No accreditation

Affiliated with: None

Psychological Orientation: Eclectic, oriented towards psycho-somatic unification. Includes holistic integration of body, mind, thought, and spirit.

Duration of Training: 4 years

Current Tuition: $3000 per year **Registration Fee:** $1500

Supervision Fee: $400 per year during the third and fourth years.

Course Fee: $50 extra for anatomy and second-year classes

Seminar Schedule: 10 weekends of class (once a month spread out over 10 months)

Average Class Size: 17 **Faculty Members:** 25

Annual Applicants: 30 **Students Accepted:** 22

Enrollment: 20 **Graduates:** 14

Program Admission Requirements:

Candidates must have a Ph.D., M.S.W., or M.A., or be involved in the healing arts. Candidates must have a license in Massage or Social

Work. Exceptions are made for those completing requirements while they are training. Additional preparatory courses may be required. Candidates must have 2 personal interviews, submit an essay, an application, 2 letters of recommendation, and a curriculum vitae.

Program Completion Requirements:

Seminar Requirements: Candidates must attend 9 process groups and didactic sessions per year; they must also attend a 3-day year-end intensive each year. Candidates also participate as an apprentice in 2 workshops during the 4 years. Commitment to 4 years of attendence and to the following: 9 Friday night process groups and Saturday didactic sessions per year and at least 2 hours of therapy a month or 100 hours of therapy by the end of the 4 years with an approved Core Energetic therapist. At least an hour of supervision per month with a faculty member is recommended. A 3-day year-end intensive is required each year in addition to participation as apprentice in 2 workshops during the 4 years and participation in group supervision in the third and fourth years. A final project demonstrating competence in Core Energetics is due at the end of the 4 years. All students will be subject to a year-end review.

Client Requirements: Minimum

Personal Analysis: Candidates must have 2 hours of therapy a month (100 hours by the end of four years) with an approved core energetic therapist.

Supervision Requirements: Candidates are encouraged to have individual supervision of at least 1 hour per month. Group supervision of 2 control cases—approximately 40 hours—is required for 2 years.

Case Presentation Requirements: One case presentation is required each month.

Thesis Requirements: A thesis is optional.

Evaluations: Evaluations are made twice a year.

Additional Information:

Core Energetics is a form of psychotherapy that recognizes and addresses 4 levels of existence—physical, emotional, mental, and spiritual. Utilizing the dimensions of energy and consciousness, the work uncovers external and internal defenses and liberates the original, or core, feelings. This process enables the individual to become a receptive, creative, vibrant being. It is a deep and powerful process that effects awareness of one's task in life and offers a means of pursuing it.

LONG ISLAND INSTITUTE OF PSYCHOANALYSIS

2201 Hempstead Turnpike
East Meadow, New York 11530
Telephone: 516-542-2006/Fax: 516-542-0026

Year Founded: 1976

Founder(s): George Nicklin, M.D.

Accredited by: New York State Board of Regents

Affiliated with: Nassau County Medical Center

Psychological Orientation: Psychoanalytic, Psychodynamic, and Family Therapy

Duration of Training: 2 to 4 years

Current Tuition: $990 per semester

Application Fee: $35

Registration Fee: $50

Supervision Fee: Varies

Course Fee: Prorated

Seminar Schedule: 15 hours per semester, 2 semesters per year.

Average Class Size: 8

Faculty Members: 56

Annual Applicants: 8

Students Accepted: 8

Enrollment: 30

Graduates: 10

Nonenrolled Students: Scholars from other fields are accepted into the seminar portion of the program.

Program Admission Requirements:

Candidates are required to have an M.D., Ph.D. in Clinical Psychology. be a C.S.W., or R.N., or be qualified clergy. One to 2 years of prior clinical experience are required, depending on the program chosen. Candidates are required to be licensed/certified before the completion of training. An application, personal interview, and letters of recommendation are required.

Program Completion Requirements:

Seminar Requirements: Candidates are required to complete 4 to 8 seminars.

Client Requirements: Candidates must conduct 100 to 200 client sessions. Candidates are paid directly by the client.

Personal Analysis: Candidates of the psychoanalytic program are required to complete 300 hours of personal analysis over 4 years with an approved analyst. Past analysis is not accepted.

Supervision Requirements: Candidates must complete 100 hours of supervision over 2 years for the clergy and family training, 100 hours over 2 years for Dynamic Psychotherapy training, and 200 hours over 4 years for Psychoanalytic training.

Case Presentation Requirements: Not applicable

Thesis Requirements: None

Evaluations: Candidates are evaluated by faculty and supervisors.

MANHATTAN INSTITUTE FOR PSYCHOANALYSIS

352 Seventh Avenue
New York, New York 10001
Telephone: 212-971-3123

Year Founded: 1981

Founder(s): Willa Cobert, Ph.D., Franklin Goldberg, Ph.D., Irwin Hirsch, Ph.D., Sheldon Kastner, Ph.D., Paul Kessel, Ph.D., Marcia Pollack, Ph.D., and Barbara Waxenberg, Ph.D.

Accredited by: Provisionally chartered by the New York State Board of Regents

Affiliated with: None

Psychological Orientation: Psychoanalysis in a contemporary interpersonal framework

Duration of Training: 4 years of classes, 4 to 5 years of supervision

Current Tuition: $200 per course, $400 per trimester, $1200 per yr (4 yrs)

Application Fee: $40

Supervision Fee: $40 per hour

Miscellaneous Fees: Psychoanalysis

Seminar Schedule: Thursday evenings—Theoretical Course: 6:30 to 8:00 P.M.; Clinical Seminar: 8:30 to 10:00 P.M. 10-week trimester system.

Average Class Size: 6-8 **Faculty Members:** 43

Nonenrolled Students: The Institute has 2 speciality clinics (The Center for the Study and Treatment of Abuse and Incest and The Center for the Study and Treatment of Compulsive and Addictive Problems) that offer seminars to professionals.

Program Admission Requirements:

Candidates must be Psychologists with a doctoral degree and a minimum of 2 years of clinical experience, Social Workers with at least 2 years post -master's degree supervised clinical experience, Nurses with a master's or doctoral degree in Psychiatric Nursing with at least 2 years postgraduate degree supervised clinical experience, or Psychiatrists with at least 2 years residency. Each applicant must be licensed/ certified in his/her respective field of practice. Personal interviews and professional letters of recommendation are required.

Program Completion Requirements:

Seminar Requirements: 4 years of courses, 2 courses per trimester (24 courses)

Client Requirements: Work with at least 2 patients in intensive psychoanalysis, beginning first year of matriculation, supervised until completion of training. Can be drawn from own practice or referred by institute low-cost clinic.

Personal Analysis: Required to be in psychoanalysis upon matriculation, for a minimum of 360 hours, of which a minimum of 300 hours are at a frequency of 3 times per week (3 times weekly to begin no later than September of second year of training). Analyst must be graduated from a psychoanalytic training institute approved by The Manhattan Institute at least 5 years prior.

Supervision Requirements: A minimum of 200 hours of supervision distributed over a minimum of 4 years.

Case Presentation Requirements: Ongoing part of clinical seminars each trimester, but no formal case presentation is required at completion of training.

Thesis Requirements: None

Evaluations: Candidates are formally evaluated at the completion of each trimester by their faculty, and annually by their supervisors, candidates receive copies of all evaluations. Annually, the Training Committee reviews all evaluations and provides feedback to each candidate.

Additional Information:

The Manhattan Institute for Psychoanalysis offers a comprehensive training program in Psychoanalysis within a contemporary interpersonal framework. The curriculum embraces both traditional psychoanalytic thought and the expansions and modifications contributed by recent theoretical advances.

The Institute is administered by co-directors and a structure of committees. Graduates and candidates are active members of these committees and, thus, have considerable input in the policies, procedures, administration, and development of the Institute.

MASTERSON INSTITUTE

60 Sutton Place South
New York, New York 10022
Telephone: 212-935-1414

Year Founded: 1986

Founder(s): James F. Masterson, M.D.

Accredited by: Accreditation Council for Continuing Medical Education (ACCME)

Affiliated with: None

Psychological Orientation: Developmental, Self and Object Relations approach to the diagnosis and treatment of the disorders of the self (personality disorders). Treatment orientation is a psychoanalytically informed Psychodynamic Psychotherapy.

Duration of Training: 3-year program

Current Tuition: $1600 per semester

Application Fee: $35 **Registration Fee:** $200

Supervision Fee: varies

Seminar Schedule: The academic year is 32 weeks long divided into two 16-week semesters. There are 3 seminars per week: a 1-hour theory seminar, a 1-hour psychopathology seminar, and a 1 1/2-hour continuous case seminar. There is an additional supervision hour (individual) each week.

Average Class Size: 12 **Faculty Members:** 10

Annual Applicants: 21 **Students Accepted:** 12

Enrollment: 12 **Graduates:** 11

Nonenrolled Students: The Institute offers seminars and study groups throughout the academic year that are open to professionals. These classes are seperate from the formal Institute training program.

Program Admission Requirements:

Matriculation as a candidate is open to licensed Psychotherapists with a professional degree from an accredited institution. Prior experience and certification are both preferred, but not required. Two individual interviews are conducted by the faculty of the Institute. A brief autobiographical sketch and 3 references are also part of the application procedure.

Program Completion Requirements:

Seminar Requirements: Candidates must complete 3 courses per semester for 3 semesters.

Client Requirements: Candidates are required to see an unspecified number of clients—enough to ensure a range of clinical experience. Candidates present patient material drawn from their own clinical practice. Candidates are asked to treat 2 patients provided by the Institute's low-cost referral service.

a requirement for acceptance into the Institute. Similarly, personal psychotherapy is strongly recommended but not required during the training program.

Supervision Requirements: Supervision is provided in all 3 years through group continuous-case study and individual and conjoint supervision for a total of 2 1/2 hours per week.

Case Presentation Requirements: Varies

Thesis Required: A formal, written case presentation is required in the third year to demonstrate integration of theory and practice.

Evaluations: Each candidate is assigned an advisor for the duration of the Certificate Program, because of the way learning takes place. The advisor is responsible for monitoring the candidate's learning and for providing evaluative feedback to the student. Advisors will formally consult with the candidates at the beginning and at the end of each semester and will provide them with the faculty's evaluation of their progress.

Additional Information:

The Masterson Institute has evolved from the work of the Masterson Group, P.C. The Group was established by James F. Masterson, M.D., in 1977 to foster the Developmental, Self and Object Relations approach to the psychotherapy of the disorders of the self (personality disorders), to teach that approach, and to foster further research. Dr. Masterson pioneered this approach through clinical research during the last 30 years. He has authored many widely acclaimed and influential works. Widespread acceptence created a demand for more teaching, which resulted in the formation of the Masterson Institute, a nonprofit organization for teaching and research.

The Masterson Institute serves as an organizational umbrella for a wide variety of teaching activities, the most intensive of which is the 3-year postgraduate Certificate Program. The Certificate Program aims to promote throrough understanding of developmental, self- and object-relations theory and its application to normal human develoment, psychopathology and psychoanalytically oriented psychotherapy. It further aims to equip therapists with the knowledge and skill required for careful differential diagnosis and for treatment of patients with disorders of the self.

METROPOLITAN INSTITUTE FOR TRAINING IN PSYCHOANALYSIS

130 West 97th Street
New York, New York 10025
Telephone: 212-864-7000/Fax: 212-932-2103

Year Founded: 1962

Founder(s): Hector Ritey, M.D.

Accredited by: New York State Board of Regents

Affiliated with: Council of Psychoanalytic Psychotherapists, Metropolitan Center for Mental Health, Metropolitan Society of Psychoanalytic Psychotherapists

Psychological Orientation: Psychoanalytic

Duration of Training: 3 years full-time or the program can be done part-time with variable duration

Current Tuition: $800 per semester.

Application Fee: $35

Course Fee: $175 part-time and $200 if nonmatriculated

Seminar Schedule: Mondays and Wednesdays at 7:00 P.M. and 9:00 P.M. Students may take 1 to 3 courses per semester.

Average Class Size: 4-8

Faculty Members: 25

Annual Applicants: 12

Students Accepted: 5

Enrollment: 4

Graduates: 4

Nonenrolled Students: Professionals only are allowed to take occasional classes.

Program Admission Requirements:

Applicants must be licensed or eligible for certification in Psychiatry, Psychology, Social Work, or Psychiatric Nursing. Those with other clinical backgrounds will be evaluated to work toward a letter of completion. Prior clinical experience will be evaluated on an individual basis. Two to 3 personal interviews, 2 letters of recommendation, a curriculum vitae, and an application form and fee are required.

Program Completion Requirements:

Seminar Requirements: 18

Client Requirements: Full-time students must conduct 8 patient sessions per semester. Part-time students must conduct 5 patient sessions per semester. Fellowships are available to experienced clinicians and there is an opportunity for all matriculants to be paid for clinical work.

Personal Analysis: Candidates must have a minimum of 300 hours of 2/week therapy for the duration of training with a graduate of a recognized psychoanalytic training institute. Past analysis is not accepted.

Supervision Requirements: Candidates must receive 120 hours of individual supervision, 40 hours each with 3 different supervisors. Candidates must engage in 3 years minimum of weekly group supervision.

Case Presentation Requirements: Every 2 years at a clinical meeting, plus a final case presentation at the end of training.

Thesis Requirements: None

Evaluations: Students receive written evaluations from supervisors and teachers. Students evaluate supervisors in writing and write also anonymous evaluations of teachers. Each student meets to discuss his or her progress at the end of each semester with the director.

M. H. ERICKSON SOCIETY FOR PSYCHOTHERAPY & HYPNOSIS

P. O. Box 1390, Madison Square Station
New York, New York 10010
Telephone: 212-628-0287/Fax: 212-874-3271

Year Founded: 1979

Founder(s):

Accredited by: New York State Board of Regents.

Affiliated with: None

Psychological Orientation: Eclectic, Ericksonian approach

Duration of Training: 100 hours

Current Tuition: $475 per 10-week segment or $2,375 per course

Registration Fee: $100

Seminar Schedule: One 2-hour session per week for 50 weeks. Semesters start September and February.

Average Class Size: 10

Faculty Members: 6

Annual Applicants: 54

Students Accepted: 54

Enrollment: 70

Graduates: 23

Program Admission Requirements:

Candidates are required to have a master's degree in a health care profession. Prior clinical experience is required. Candidates who are state licensed receive a diploma; candidates without a license receive a letter of completion. Candidates must be health care professionals in practice.

Program Completion Requirements:

Seminar Requirements: Candidates must attend 48 of the 50 sessions.

Client Requirements: Not applicable

Personal Analysis: Not applicable.

Supervision Requirements: Not applicable.

Case Presentation Requirements: Not applicable.

Thesis Requirements: Candidates are required to present a written case detailing client's progress through 5 sessions of Hypnotherapy.

Evaluations: Evaluations are made by a committee of faculty members.

Additional Information:

The NYSEPH Training Program has evolved into a program that models Dr. Erickson's thinking and the techniques of his students, Sid Rosen, Jane Parsons-Fein, Rita Sherr, and Jeffrey Feldman. Ten years ago, the 4 practitioners met to discuss Erickson's ideas. They decided to form a training program that would provide students with a comprehensive understanding of Erickson's thinking and a long enough period of time in which to consistently and systematically integrate his approaches into their practices. Erickson's thinking takes a long time to assimilate, so the faculty built a structure that would enable students to comfortably and gracefully integrate the essence of his work. NYSEPH continues to seek flexibility, change, and new structures within its organization to create and expand programs that will maintain the rigor and vigor of Erickson's approaches. The NYSEPH program is different from the way Erickson taught. There was no Ericksonian Society when Erickson was alive, as he had an aversion to organizations. He taught informally. His students would come and go, studying with him for varying lengths of time according to their interest and life circumstances, not for a specified time period as established by NYSEPH. Furthermore, he did not have students practice in front of him, nor did he encourage group interaction or community. Although NYSEPH's training program is different from Erickson's form of training, the variations in style—and, in fact, the variations among the 4 instructors—all express his philosophy that there is no one effective method of psychotherapy. Each therapist and training program should develop a unique way rather than be a clone of Milton Erickson.

NATIONAL INSTITUTE FOR THE PSYCHOTHERAPIES

330 West 58th Street, Suite 200
New York, New York 10019
Telephone: 212-582-1566

Year Founded: 1972

Founder(s): Henry Grayson, Ph.D., Chair, James L. Fosshage, Ph.D., Kenneth A. Frank, Ph.D., Clemens A. Loew, Henry Lowenheim, Ph.D.

Accredited by: New York State Board of Regents

Affiliated with: None

Psychological Orientation: Psychoanalytic, Object Relations, Self Psychology, Ego Psychology, Interpersonal Theories, Integrative Nonanalytic Modalities

Duration of Training: 4-year program leading to a certificate in Psychoanalysis and Comprehensive Psychotherapy.

Current Tuition: $290 per course per semester ($1740 annually)

Application Fee: $50

Supervision Fee: $45 per individual session, $20 per group session

Miscellaneous Fees: $115 consultation fee

Course Fee: Minimal fees for 3 required June semester courses

Seminar Schedule: Three courses per semester are offered sequentially from 8 A.M. to 1 P.M., one day per week (same day throughout the 4 years of study). Courses are 1 1/2 hours each and meet for 15 weeks.

Average Class Size: 12

Faculty Members: 100

Annual Applicants: 30

Students Accepted: 15

Enrollment: 14

Graduates: 9

Nonenrolled Students: There are June workshops and a C.E. program that professionals can attend.

Program Admission Requirements:

Candidates must be Ph.D. Psychologists, M.D. Psychiatrists, M.S.W. Social Workers, or master's degree Mental Health Nurses. Candidates must have a minimum of 1 year of postdegree experience in a clinical setting. Candidates must be eligible for New York State certification. Completed applications must include 3 letters of recommendation, college and graduate school transcripts, and 2 individual and 1 group interview.

Program Completion Requirements:

Seminar Requirements: Candidates must complete 24 courses (3 per semester). They must complete 1 continuing education (CE) workshop and 1 colloquium per year.

Client Requirements: Candidates must conduct 10 client sessions per week. Trainees are reimbursed for each session. Opportunities for referrals to graduates are also available.

Personal Analysis: Candidates must have 350 hours of 2-time-a-week psychotherapy with a graduate of an approved 4-year postgraduate psychoanalytic training institute, concurrent with the 4-year training program. Past analysis is not accepted.

Supervision Requirements: Candidates are required to have 40 hours of individual supervision and 40 hours of group supervision for each of the first 3 years, and 34 hours of individual and 34 hours of group supervision in the 4th year. During the third and fourth years, candidates may elect to have 2 individual supervisors rather than an individual and a group experience. A control case is required.

Case Presentation Requirements: (see Thesis requirements)

Thesis Requirements: A final project (paper about 25 pages) is required to demonstrate the candidate's abitity to integrate clinical and theoretical material.

Evaluations: Evaluation meetings, where supervisors and faculty meet to discuss the candidate's progress, are held twice a year. Candidates are informed of the content and recommendations of these meetings by their advisors. Candidates also have the opportunity to evaluate their instructors and supervisors.

Additional Information:

The training program promotes the development of a solid theoretical foundation in psychodynamic processes, while maintaining a spirit of openness and eclecticism. After graduation, candidates are invited to become active members of the NIP Professional Association to continue their involvement with our professional community.

NEW HOPE GUILD CENTERS TRAINING PROGRAMS

1777 East 21st Street
Brooklyn, New York 11229
Telephone: 718-252-4200/Fax: 718-258-0139

Year Founded: 1973

Founder(s): Sherman O. Schacter, M.D. and Jeanette Levitt, M.A.

Accredited by: New York State Office of Mental Health

Affiliated with: New Hope Guild Centers

Psychological Orientation: Child and Adolescent Therapy Training Program (Psychoanalytic)

Duration of Training: 3 years

Current Tuition: No cost

Seminar Schedule: 12 hours of class per week on Tuesdays from 7 P.M. -9 P.M. (meets at faculty members' offices). Classes start the day after Labor Day and end the last Tuesday in June.

Average Class Size: 10

Faculty Members: 15

Annual Applicants: 19

Students Accepted: 10

Enrollment: 10

Graduates: 4

Nonenrolled Students: New Hope Guild Centers offer workshops that professionals are welcome to attend.

Program Admission Requirements:

Candidates must have a doctorate in Psychology or A.B.D., M.S.W., M.D. with psychiatric training, or be Psychiatric Nurse master's level. Prior clinical experience is preferable, but not required. Prior certification or licensing or preparation for licensing is required. Personal analysis is required. The requirements for admission include a 3-step interview: the first with a director, the second with a faculty member, and the third with the Clinic Director; 3 letters of recommendation; a curriculum vitae, and a copy of a license or a letter from a graduate program indicating when the degree is to be completed.

Program Completion Requirements:

Seminar Requirements: All seminars must be completed. This is a lock-step program.

Client Requirements: Candidates must see 5 to 6 children per week, plus allocate an hour for collaterals with parents. Candidates must conduct 180 client sessions in the second year and 200 hours in the third year. A $100 per month stipend is paid in the third year, when the 180-hour requirement is met.

Personal Analysis: Candidates must have 200 hours of analysis with a graduate of an analytically oriented training program over a 2-year period. Past analysis may be accepted, but if a supervisor believes that a candidate needs further treatment, the candidate must re-enter treatment to complete the program. It is acceptable if the analyst sees the candidate as a training case at an Institute.

Supervision Requirements: Candidates must have 144 hours of supervision over a 3-year period.

Case Presentation Requirements: Case presentations are only required if a faculty member requests it for a class.

Thesis Requirements: None

Evaluations: Each faculty member evaluates each candidate after the completion of the course. Each student evaluates each faculty member. Each supervisor writes evaluations at the end of the year. The director evaluates them all. If there is a problem, a committee reviews all of them.

Additional Information:

New Hope Guild Centers have a 40-year history of offering services to their communities. By providing training, New Hope offers a service to the professional community who, in turn, gives needed help to the New Hope Guild communitees. All beginning candidates are given a $50 allowance to buy materials. When the 180-hour requirement is completed at the end of the second year, a monthly stipend is paid in the third year. A certificate is awarded at the completion of all requirements. The program has an affiliated Graduate Society and has a quarterly newsletter. There is no charge for any part of this training program.

NEW YORK FREUDIAN SOCIETY

200 East End Avenue
New York, New York 10128
Telephone: 212 348-1230/Fax: 718-268-6617

Year Founded: 1959

Accredited by: New York State Board of Regents

Affiliated with: Provisional Society of the International Psychoanalytical Association (IPA)

Psychological Orientation: Programs in Adult and Child Psychoanalysis, Freudian Psychoanalytic Theory, Ego Psychology, Object Relations Theory, modern contributions

Duration of Training: Candidates take 2 courses per semester for a total of 4 years. Weekly supervision of analytic patients (2) is required for a minimum total of 200 hours.

Current Tuition: $300 per semester

Application Fee: $30

Registration Fee: $50

Supervision Fee: Varies

Miscellaneous Fees: $15 candidate organization fee

Seminar Schedule: Two 15-week seminars per semester. Meetings are held on Monday nights.

Average Class Size: 6

Faculty Members: 46

Annual Applicants: 28

Students Accepted: 21

Enrollment: 74

Graduates: 23

Nonenrolled Students: Professionals may take first year courses only.

Program Admission Requirements:

Candidates must have a master's degree or higher in Psychology, Social Work, Psychiatric Medicine, Psychiatric Nursing, or another appropriate field of study from institutions acceptable to the training committee. Prior clinical experience is suggested but not required. One may be accepted as a candidate but must be liscensed or certified in one of the mental health professions to receive a certificate of completed training. Candidates must be at least 25 years of age. An application interview and letters of recommendation are required as part of the application.

Program Completion Requirements:

Seminar Requirements: Candidates must complete 16 courses.

Client Requirements: Candidates must see 2 patients with 2 supervisors in the first 3 years for a Psychoanalytic Psychotherapy certificate. They must see 2 patients with 2 supervisors in the second 3 years for a certificate of completion in Psychoanalysis.

Personal Analysis: Candidates must enter 4-time-a-week analysis upon entry into the program. No prior treatment is required. Prior analysis or ongoing analysis may be accepted by the Training Committee upon request of the candidate. The analyst and analysis must be approved by the IPA.

Supervision Requirements: Candidates must work with 2 supervised control cases for a minimum of 4 times per week. Candidates must receive a minimum of 200 hours of weekly supervision with 2 different supervisors who have NYFS training.

Case Presentation Requirements: Candidates must present a case at the end of their course of study when they are ready to graduate.

Thesis Requirements: None

Evaluations: "Readiness for Control" interviews are conducted after 8 courses are completed to determine the candidate's ability to begin a supervised treatment of an analytic patient. Candidates present vignettes from treatment and demonstrate their ability to combine theory with clinical application.

Additional Information:

Upon graduation the candidate is eligible for membership in the International Psychoanalytic Association. Candidates also may participate in ongoing postgraduate seminars with highly trained, eminent Psychoanalysts who are represented in the Society's membership.

NEW YORK PSYCHOANALYTIC INSTITUTE

247 East 82nd Street
New York, New York 10028
Telephone: 212-879-6900/Fax: 212-879-0588

Year Founded: 1931

Founder(s): Dr. Abraham Brill

Accredited by: Board on Professional Standards of the American Psychoanalytic Association

Affiliated with: None

Psychological Orientation: Classical (Freudian)

Duration of Training: Varies (a minimum of 4 years and an average of 6 years)

Current Tuition: Based on courses taken

Application Fee: $170

Supervision Fee: $1600

Miscellaneous Fees: Matriculation & graduation fees

Seminar Schedule: Evenings

Average Class Size: 7

Faculty Members: 90

Annual Applicants: 10

Students Accepted: 4

Enrollment: 45

Graduates: 2

Nonenrolled Students: Analysts from other institutes have occasionally taken classes in the Child-Adolescent Program.

Program Admission Requirements:

Candidates must have an M.D., Ph.D., or Psy.D. in Clinical Psychology, or a D.S.W. in Social Work. M.D.'s must have 2 years of accredited Psychiatric Residency; Ph.D.'s and Psy.D.'s must have comparable clinical experience. Candidates must be licensed to practice in New York State. In-depth personal interviews and letters of recommendation are required for admission.

Program Completion Requirements:

Seminar Requirements: Candidates must complete approximately 6 to 8 courses each year.

Client Requirements: Candidates must conduct a minimum of 3 supervised analyses; the average is 4 to 5. Payment provisions are privately arranged.

Personal Analysis: Candidates must enter a personal analysis with a training and supervising analyst. The duration varies.

Supervision Requirements: Candidates must receive supervision on a minimum of 3 control cases, with 4 to 5 cases being the average.

Case Presentation Requirements: Not applicable

Thesis Requirements: A thesis is required.

Evaluations: Written evaluations are conducted by every course instructor, by each supervisor, and by the faculty advisors. The candidate graduates when the Students Committee and the Educational Committee determine that the candidate has achieved an expected level of competence to practice independently.

Additional Information:

The New York Psychoanalytic Society is the oldest psychoanalytic organization in the United States. It was founded on February 11, 1911, by Dr. Abraham Brill, who since 1908 had been meeting with a small group of Psychiatrists, to discuss the revolutionary discoveries of Freud. Among the 15 charter members of The New York Analytic Society, the most active and well-known were Brill and Clarence P. Oberndorf, M.D. Brill also lectured extensively on Freud's theories at the meetings of the Neurology and Psychiatry Section of the New York Academy of Medicine, as well as at the other scientific forums throughout the city. Brill's Freud translations, together with the prolific writings of other early members of the New York Society, brought psychoanalysis to a widening audience of American readers. As the demand for psychoanalytic knowledge and training steadily increased, the members of The New York Psychoanalytic Society and their Educational Committee established The New York Psychoanalytic Institute on September 24, 1931.

NEW YORK SCHOOL FOR PSYCHOANALYTIC PSYCHOTHERAPY

200 West 57th Street
New York, New York 10019
Telephone: 212-245-7045

Year Founded: 1978

Founder(s): Edwin Fancher, Miriam Pierce, Rosalie Korte, and Jane Hall

Accredited by: New York Board of Regents

Affiliated with: Council of Psychoanalytic Psychotherapists

Psychological Orientation: Freudian Ego Psychology, Developmental, Object Relations Theory

Duration of Training: The Psychotherapy Program is 3 years. Advanced Training in Psychoanalysis is an additional 2 years.

Current Tuition: $400 per semester

Application Fee: $30

Supervision Fee: $50

Seminar Schedule: 2 classes of 1 1/2-hour usually held on Monday evenings from 6:30 to 9:30 P.M. or 7 to 10 P.M.

Average Class Size: 8

Faculty Members: 22

Annual Applicants: 25

Students Accepted: 15

Enrollment: 12

Program Admission Requirements:

Candidates must be licensed or licensable Social Workers, Psychologists, Psychiatric Nurses, or Psychiatrists. Some prior clinical experience is useful. Two personal interviews and 2 letters of reference are required for admission.

Program Completion Requirements:

Client Requirements: Candidates must work with 2 cases for 50 hours each.

Personal Analysis: Candidates must have 300 hours of personal analysis with a psychoanalytically oriented therapist. Past analysis with a psychoanalytically oriented therapist may be accepted.

Supervision Requirements: Candidates must have 100 hours of supervision, of 2 cases (50 hours each).

Case Presentation Requirements: Case presentations are required in the clinical case seminars. Students present an average of 5 times per semester.

Thesis Requirements: None

Evaluations: A final case presentation for graduation is heard by a committee. Clinical competency is based on the candidate's ability to engage the patient, to form a treatment alliance, to grasp the patient's dynamics, to handle transference and countertransference, and to utilize supervision. Candidates are evaluated throughout the course of training. Each class requires an exam or paper.

Additional Information:

The New York School for Psychoanalytic Psychotherapy's 3-year curriculum offers a course of study linking traditional Freudian concepts to contemporary Ego Psychology as developed by Anna Freud, Hartmann, Spitz, and Mahler. NYSPP offers small, personalized classes in New York City and on Long Island.

PSYCHOANALYTIC INSTITUTE OF THE POSTGRADUATE CENTER FOR MENTAL HEALTH

124 East 28th Street
New York, New York 10016
Telephone: 212-576-4168/Fax: 212-576-4198

Year Founded: 1945

Founder(s): Lewis Wolberg, M.D., and Arlene Wolberg, M.S.S.W.

Accredited by: New York State Board of Regents

Affiliated with: None

Psychological Orientation: Classical and ontemporary Freudian theory, major alternative analytic theories

Duration of Training: 4 years in the Adult Psychoanalytic Training Program. Duration varies for the Child and Adolescent Psychoanalytic Training Program, the Counseling Program, and others.

Current Tuition: $600 per year or 500 patient hours in the Adult Clinic

Application Fee: $50

Registration Fee: $25

Miscellaneous Fees: $25 annual library fee

Seminar Schedule: Three classes per trimester that meet Tuesdays from 8:30 A.M. to 12:45 P.M. Each trimester is approximately 12 weeks in length.

Average Class Size: 9

Faculty Members: 45

Annual Applicants: 17

Students Accepted: 10

Enrollment: 10

Graduates: 7

Program Admission Requirements:

Candidates must be a Psychiatrist, Psychologist, Clinical Social Worker, or a Psychiatric Nurse. Candidates must have 1 or 2 years of supervised professional experience, depending on their degree. Candidates must be licensed (certified in New York State).

Program Completion Requirements:

Seminar Requirements: Candidates must complete 31 seminars.

Client Requirements: Candidates must conduct 500 client sessions per year in lieu of tuition.

Personal Analysis: Candidates must receive 400 hours of personal analysis, 3 times per week, beginning 1 year prior to admission. The analyst must be from the Institute list. No prior analysis is accepted.

Supervision Requirements: Candidates receive 300 to 400 hours of supervision, 2 interviews, and 1 overall per week.

Case Presentations Requirements: A case presentation is made in the fourth year of training on a patient seen in analysis 3 times a week for 2 years.

Thesis Requirements: None

Evaluations: Candidates are evaluated by their supervisors twice a year and are reviewed annually by the Training and Evaluation Committee. The committee approves readiness to proceed to the next year of training or, in the fourth year, to graduate.

Additional Information:

The Psychoanalytic Institute includes the core adult psychoanalytic Training Program and specialty programs in Child and Adolescent treatment, Family and Couples treatment, Analytic Group Therapy, and supervision of the psychoanalytic process. In addition, the Institute offers programs in Pastoral Counseling and an Advanced training program for mental health professionals with limited clinical experience. The faculty and candidates come from the disciplines of Psychiatry, Psychology, Social Work, and Psychiatric Nursing, and cooperate in a multidisciplinary atmosphere in which no distinction is made among the disciplines.

Candidates in all of the programs benefit from the Institute's "teaching hospital" model, which enables the Institute to offer candidates the opportunity for extensive work with diverse kinds of patients through accredited, community-based mental health clinics. The Emil Gutheil Library, established in 1947, is a leading psychiatric library in New York City and provides students and faculty with a unique source of books and periodicals on psychoanalysis and related mental health subjects. The Institute offers candidates in all of its programs the opportunity to attend case conferences, scientific lectures, and workshops, and to participate in a stimulating collegial atmosphere with a community of intellectually and socially committed professionals.

PSYCHOANALYTIC TRAINING INSTITUTE OF THE NEW YORK COUNSELING & GUIDANCE SERVICE

160 West End Avenue
New York, New York 10023
Telephone: 212-362-1086/Fax: 212-877-9204

Year Founded: 1977

Founder(s): Alan Grossman, C.S.W., B.C.D.

Accredited by: New York State Department of Education

Affiliated with: None

Psychological Orientation: Psychoanalytic Psychotherapy

Duration of Training: 3 years

Current Tuition: $350 per trimester ($1050 annually)

Application Fee: $25 **Supervision Fee:** $30

Seminar Schedule: 2 classes every Wednesday from 6:45 P.M. to 10:00 A.M.

Average Class Size: 10 **Faculty Members:** 25

Annual Applicants: 20 **Students Accepted:** 10

Enrollment: 16 **Graduates:** 3

Nonenrolled Students: Professionals may take the occasional class.

Program Admission Requirements:

Candidates must have a Ph.D., M.S.W., M.D., or C.C.S. No prior clinical experience is required. Candidates must be licensable in a mental health profession. Two interviews and 3 letters of recommendation are required for admission.

Program Completion Requirements:

Seminar Requirements: Candidates are required to complete 27 seminars.

Client Requirements: Candidates are required to conduct 5 client sessions per week for a total of 500 hours in 3 years.

Personal Analysis: Candidates are required to complete 300 hours of personal analysis with a Psychoanalytic Analyst. Past analysis is accepted.

Supervision Requirements: Weekly supervision is required throughout the 3-year training period.

Case Presentation Requirements: One case presentation is required.

Thesis Requirements: A clinical paper is presented to a 3-person committee.

Evaluations: Evaluatons are conducted at the end of each trimester by each teacher and twice yearly by each supervisor.

TRAINING INSTITUTE OF THE NATIONAL PSYCHOLOGICAL ASSOCIATION FOR PSYCHOANALYSIS (NPAP)

150 West 13th Street
New York, New York 10011
Telephone: 212-924-7440 /Fax: 212-989-7543

Year Founded: 1948

Founder(s): Dr. Theodore Reik

Accredited by: New York State Board of Regents (1967), NAAP

Affiliated with: National Association for Psychoanalysis, Inc.; Council of Psychoanalytic Psychotherapists

Psychological Orientation: Comprehensive program of Psychoanalytic training.

Duration of Training: Each member-in-training (MIT) proceeds at his or her own pace for an average of 6 to 10 years.

Current Tuition: Dependents on the number of courses taken each trimester

Application Fee: $25

Registration Fee: $75 per year

Supervision Fee: Individually contracted with NPAP

Miscellaneous Fees: Individual training analysis

Course Fee: 24 courses at $200 per course

Seminar Schedule: There are 25 basic courses, 8 on each of 3 levels of training. Courses are 12 weeks long, 1 1/2 hours in length. They are given in the evenings at 7 P.M. and 9 P.M.

Average Class Size: 7

Faculty Members: 79

Annual Applicants: 37

Students Accepted: 18

Enrollment: 185

Graduates: 17

Nonenrolled Students: NPAP welcomes students with training in tridisciplines, as well as people with advanced training in any helping profession, academic discipline, or the arts (a master's degree is required). All taking classes must be accepted into the training program.

Program Admission Requirements:

Candidates must have a master's degree in any professional field of the arts and sciences. Candidates must be 25 years of age, submit transcripts of undergraduate and graduate study, have 2 personal enrollment interviews, and submit 2 letters of recommendation.

Program Completion Requirements:

Seminar Requirements: Candidates must complete 24 courses and pass 3 evaluation oral exams.

Client Requirements: Candidates must conduct 360 client sessions plus 150 hours of control analysis. Payment is individually contracted with clients. At the matriculation level (second level) of training, members-in-training are eligible to receive referrals from TRCC.

Personal Analysis: Candidates must complete a minimum of 450 hours of personal analysis with an NPAP analyst. Past analysis is accepted with analysts approved by the Dean of Training.

Supervision Requirements: Candidates receive supervision throughout clinical practice plus 150 hours of control supervision of 2 control cases.

Case Presentation Requirements: Two case presentation seminars are required, as well as a case presentation for graduation.

Thesis Requirements: None

Evaluations: Evaluations are made by all instructors and supervisors. As the student progresses through the training program s/he must pass 3 oral evaluations to graduate: Matriculation Evaluation, Readiness-for-Control, and Case Presentation.

Additional Information:

NPAP is the oldest nonmedical Psychoanalytic Training Institute in the United States. NPAP offers a unique and comprehensive curriculum in the theory and technique of Psychoanalysis from a broad range of perspectives. NPAP's Board of Trustees is elected from the membership and is responsible for the administration of the training program.

The training program is based upon a system of progressive evaluation which is designed to provide each member-in-training (MIT) with guidance on an individual basis, so as to coordinate the advancement of course work with the progress of personal analysis and the commencement of supervised practice. For MITs on the matriculation level (second level), the Theodor Reik Consultation Center (TRCC) offers a referral service. Working with clients received from TRCC provides the MIT with clinical experience as he or she begins supervised psychotherapy at the RFC level (third level) as he or she begins an analytic practice.

WASHINGTON SQUARE INSTITUTE FOR PSYCHOTHERAPY AND MENTAL HEALTH

41 East 11th Street
New York, New York 10003
Telephone: 212-477-2600/Fax: 212-477-2040

Year Founded: 1960

Founder(s): Gerd H. Fenchel, Ph.D., Edwin Fancher, M.A., and Anthony Lenzo, C.S.W.

Accredited by: The New York State Education Department, The National Association for the Advancement of Psychoanalysis

Affiliated with: Council of Psychoanalytic Psychotherapists

Psychological Orientation: Psychoanalysis, Ego Psychology, Object Relations

Duration of Training: 3 to 4 years

Current Tuition: $3,500

Application Fee: $15 **Registration Fee:** $30

Miscellaneous Fees: $17.50 for certificate

Seminar Schedule: 2 nights a week (Monday and Wednesday) and 2 summer courses.

Average Class Size: 15 **Faculty Members:** 13

Annual Applicants: 25 **Students Accepted:** 25

Enrollment: 65 **Graduates:** 5

Nonenrolled Students: First year classes may be audited.

Program Admission Requirements:

Candidates must have a minimum of a master's degree in a traditional Mental Health Field, Human Relations, or Nursing. Other fields will be considered. Prior clinical experience is not required, but it is desirable .Prior certification is also desirable but not required. An interview, application blank, and autobiography are required for admission.

Program Completion Requirements:

Seminar Requirements: Candidates must complete 469 class hours.

Client Requirements: Candidates must work with 7 clients. They will receive a stipend of $5 per hour. Client referrals are only given to students affiliating themselves with the Treatment Center.

Personal Analysis: Candidates must have a minimum of 300 hours of personal analysis for the duration of the training. Past analysis is not accepted.

Supervision Requirements: Candidates must have a minimum of 350 hours of supervision for the duration of training. Two control cases are required for advanced classes in Psychoanalysis.

Case Presentation Requirements: Case presentations are required.

Thesis Requirements: None

Evaluations: Candidates are evaluated by each teacher. A supervisory evaluation is performed 2 times a year.

Additional Information:

The Washington Square Institute publishes the *Issue in Psychology* Journal and a series of monographs on Group Therapy. Faculty and supervisors are graduate analysts. On a weekly basis, 1600 sessions are conducted in the Institute's 18,000-square-foot facility.

WESTCHESTER CENTER FOR THE STUDY OF PSYCHOANALYSIS & PSYCHOTHERAPY

29 Sterling Avenue
White Plains, New York 10606
Telephone:

Year Founded: 1974

Founder(s): Sabert Besescu, Bernard Fisher, Edward Gaughran, Alan Grey, Oscar Hyman, Dale Ortmeyer, Wm. Silverberg, Paul Stark, and Herbert Zucker

Accredited by: New York State Board of Regents

Affiliated with: None

Psychological Orientation: Pluralistic—Psychoanalysis and Psychoanalytic Psychotherapy

Duration of Training: 4 years

Current Tuition: $250 per course ($1500 per year)

Application Fee: $40

Registration Fee: $100

Supervision Fee: $50

Course Fee: $250

Seminar Schedule: 2 classes per trimester, 1 hour and 40 minutes each, for 11 sessions. A total of 6 classes per academic year. Classes meet Tuesday nights from 7 P.M. to 10 P.M.

Average Class Size: 9

Faculty Members: 41

Annual Applicants: 12

Students Accepted: 8

Enrollment: 31 **Graduates:** 8

Nonenrolled Students: Graduates may audit courses with the permission of the instructor and the class.

Program Admission Requirements:

Candidates must have an M.D. in Psychiatry, a Ph.D. in Psychology, or an M.S.W. in Social Work. They must have 2 years of supervised clinical individual psychotherapeutic experience, at least a year of which must be with adults. Candidates must be licensed or eligible for state licensure. Personal analysis and supervision are required. Two personal interviews and 4 letters of reference are required for admission.

Program Completion Requirements:

Seminar Requirements: 24 seminars are required.

Client Requirements: Candidates must complete 320 hours of treatment service work under faculty supervision. Fees are payable to WCSPP.

Personal Analysis: Candidates must undergo one year of personal analysis with a faculty analyst or an analyst approved by the faculty, who has been certified for a minimum of 5 years.

Supervision Requirements: Candidates must complete 160 hours of supervision over a 4-year period.

Case Presentation Requirements: Not applicable

Thesis Requirements: None

Evaluations: Candidates receive detailed written evaluations by their supervisors, signed by both supervisor and candidate, and shorter written evaluations by their instructors. Evaluations are available to the candidate. The candidate's progress is reviewed by the Committee on Evaluation.

Additional Information:

The Westchester Center is an eclectic institute. Faculty members represent a variety of theoretical orientations, and the seminars offer an introduction to the different theoretical contributions in the fields of Psychoanalysis and Psychotherapy. Candidates are free to choose their supervisors from the faculty and are encouraged to explore different theoretical orientations. The majority of faculty members are also affiliated with other recognized analytic training institutes in the metropolitan area.

WESTCHESTER INSTITUTE FOR TRAINING IN PSYCHOLOGY & PSYCHOANALYSIS

2 Sarles Street, Box 89
Mount Kisco, New York 10549
Telephone: 914-666-0161

Year Founded: 1960

Founder(s): H. Holt, M.D. and L.R. Hartley, Jr., M.Div.

Accredited by: 1977 Absolute Charter from the New York State Education Department, N.A.A.P., A.B.A.C.

Affiliated with: Hudson River Counseling Service

Psychological Orientation: Existential Psychoanalysis, traditional and modern Psychoanalytic theories are explored in the light of an existential understanding of the human condition.

Duration of Training: 4 years

Current Tuition: $1200 per trimester

Application Fee: $75

Supervision Fee: $65 per session

Miscellaneous Fees: Personal analysis

Seminar Schedule: 6 classes each trimester for 4 years

Average Class Size: 10

Faculty Members: 22

Annual Applicants: 10

Students Accepted: 8

Enrollment: 8

Graduates: 5

Nonenrolled Students: In special cases, individuals are permitted to attend some classes without enrolling in the program.

Program Admission Requirements:

Candidates must have a master's degree in a field related to mental health (including Education and the Arts). Prior clinical experience is preferred, but not required. Candidates must have a personal interview and submit a brief essay, transcripts, and 6 letters of recommendation to the Admissions Committee.

Program Completion Requirements:

Seminar Requirements: Candidates must complete 72 seminars.

Client Requirements: Candidates must complete 400 client sessions. If clients are seen through the Hudson River Counseling Service, 40-55% of their fee is applied to the candidates' supervision or tuition fees.

Personal Analysis: Candidates must complete 300 hours of personal analysis with an approved analyst over the 4 years. Past analysis is not accepted for the training analysis.

Supervision Requirements: Candidates receive 200 hours of supervision over 4 years. One control case must be seen for 50 hours.

Case Presentation Requirements: Candidates present cases approximately twice each year, and a final case presentation that includes a written report of a case demonstrating a working understanding of resistances, transference, and countertransference is required.

Thesis Requirements: None

Evaluations: Candidates are evaluated for readiness for clinical work by the end of the first year, and readiness for control analysis during the third or fourth year of training. The Executive Committee makes a final evaluation of readiness for graduation.

WOMEN'S THERAPY CENTRE INSTITUTE

80 East 11th Street, Room 101
New York, New York
Telephone: 212-420-1974

Year Founded: 1981

Founder(s): Carol Bloom, Luise Eichenbaum, Susie Orbach

Accredited by: Application to New York State Board of Regents

Affiliated with: The Women's Therapy Centre, London, England

Psychological Orientation: Psychoanalytic—British Object Relations, American Interpersonal, Feminist

Duration of Training: 3 years

Current Tuition: $1600 per semester

Application Fee: $50

Seminar Schedule: 2 classes (theory and clinical practice) 1 evening per week for a combined class time of 3 hours

Average Class Size: 12 **Faculty Members:** 8

Annual Applicants: 20 **Students Accepted:** 16

Enrollment: **Graduates:** 7

Nonenrolled Students: Professionals and others in clinical practice may take classes at the Centre.

Program Admission Requirements:

Candidates must hold a graduate degree in a mental health profession. Applicants from other disciplines with strong aptitude and experience are also accepted. Candidates must have some clinical experience. Certification and licensure is recommended. Candidates must have had a minimum of 3 years of 2/week Psychoanalytic Psychotherapy. Candidates must submit a biographical essay and 2 letters of recommendation, and undergo 2 interviews.

Program Completion Requirements:

Seminar Requirements: Candidates must complete 3 hours of classes per week for 30 weeks each year for a total of 270 hours.

Client Requirements: Not applicable

Personal Analysis: Candidates must receive 270 hours of twice weekly Psychoanalytic Psychotherapy over 3 years. Past analysis is accepted.

Supervision Requirements: Weekly supervision is required throughout the 3-year training for a total of 120 hours.

Case Presentation Requirements: Approximately 1 case presentation per semester is required.

Thesis Requirements: Candidates have their choice in the last 2 seminars of study to do a term paper or an original piece of theoretical work.

Evaluations: Evaluations are submitted by 2 supervisors and by faculty at least 2 times during the 3 year course.

Additional Information:

The Women's Therapy Centre Institute focuses its original clinical and theoretical work on the detailed examination of the impact of gender on psychic structure, and on a woman's relationship to food, eating, and her body.

The Women's Therapy Centre Institute offers programs for the public and practitioners including short courses, workshops, seminars, a lecture series, and speakouts on a variety of topics relating to women's eating and body image issues. The WTCI operates a nationwide referral service. The Women's Therapy Centre in London (founded in 1976) is a sister organization that serves 2000 women and their families each year.

The WTCI offers a 3-year, postgraduate training program in Psychoanalytic Psychotherapy. The program enlists the work of the British Independent School of Object Relations, the American Interpersonalists, and contemporary feminist theorists to create a framework for understanding psychic life in its developmental, social, and gendered dimensions. The training draws on the work of social historians and critics to elaborate a perspective that sees individual subjectivity as inseperable from the wider culture. Our goal is to provide candidates with an integration of developments within Psychoanalysis, from Freud to the most current evolutions of theory and technique.

GESTALT TRAINING CENTER - BOONE, N.C.

204 Hillandale Drive
Boone, North Carolina 28607
Telephone: 704-264-2598

Year Founded: 1975

Founder(s): John P. Mulgrew, Ph.D.

Accredited by: No accreditation **Affiliated with:** None

Psychological Orientation: Gestalt Therapy

Duration of Training: 2 years to obtain a certificate of completion

Current Tuition: $1200 per year

Application Fee: $75 **Supervision Fee:** $80

Miscellaneous Fees: $1000 for week-long intensive

Course Fee: $100 days, $75 students; $300 weekends, $275 students

Seminar Schedule: Year-long meets for 6 weekends from 6 P.M. Friday until 12 P.M. Sunday

Average Class Size: 13 **Faculty Members:** 1

Annual Applicants: 17 **Students Accepted:** 12

Enrollment: 12 **Graduates:** 12

Program Admission Requirements:

Candidates must have a master's degree in a helping profession in a mental health field. Candidates must have had experience as a Psychotherapist for at least a year. Candidates must submit 3 letters of recommendation. A personal interview may be required.

Program Completion Requirements:

Seminar Requirements: Candidates must complete 2 years of weekend workshops in a planned and directed Gestalt Therapy training program offered at the Institute.

Client Requirements: Not applicable

Personal Analysis: Not applicable

Supervision Requirements: Candidates receive supervision for 100 hours over 2 years.

Case Presentation Requirements: Candidates work with clients "live" during training.

Thesis Requirements: None

Evaluations: Candidates receive ongoing evaluations as they progress through the program.

Additional Information:

The program is 25% didactic and 75% experiential. It offers workshops in Gestalt Therapy for the general public and intensive training for advanced professionals and students.

CENTER FOR FAMILY & BRIEF THERAPIES

Office in the Park, 24400 Highpoint Road, Suite 9
Beachwood, Ohio 44122
Telephone: 216-360-0776

Year Founded: 1989

Founder(s): Riley Lipman, Ph.D., and Frances G. Friedman, Ph.D.

Accredited by: No accreditation

Affiliated with: The faculty are affiliated with local hospitals, including Mt. Sinai Medical Center and The Gestalt Institute of Cleveland.

Psychological Orientation: Integrated Family Systems and Integrated Brief

Therapy Orientation. Includes training in methods derived from Structural, Strategic, and Bowenian therapies, and from Solution-Focused and Cognitive-Behavioral Approaches.

Duration of Training: Duration ranges from 1-day, 2-day, and week -long workshops, to a year-long externship.

Current Tuition: Varies **Course Fee:** Varies

Seminar Schedule: Workshop topics provide beginner, intermediate, and advanced training in both general skills development and on particular topics, including working with chemically dependent families and clients, working with men, and Pediatric Family Therapy.

Average Class Size: 10 **Faculty Members:** 5

Program Admission Requirements:

Candidates must hold or be training toward a professional degree in Psychology, Psychiatry, Social Work, Psychiatric Nursing, or Counseling. Candidates taking advanced level courses may be required to present letters of recommendation.

Program Completion Requirements:

Seminar Requirements: The number of seminars required varies by the program or workshop.

Client Requirements: The number of client sessions varies.

Personal Analysis: Not applicable

Supervision Requirements: Supervision requirements vary with each program or workshop.

Case Presentation Requirements: Live and videotaped supervision of cases is required in some programs.

Thesis Requirements: None

Evaluations: Evaluation of trainees is generally informal, based on consensus of faculty and on trainees' participation and live supervision, if applicable. Evaluation of the faculty by trainees is done or anonymous evaluations.

Additional Information:

The Center for Family and Brief Therapies was established to provide state-of-the-art psychological therapy and comprehensive professional training in Family Systems and Brief Therapy approaches. The faculty members have taught around the country and at local Institutes, such as the Gestalt Institute of Cleveland and the Mandel School of Social Work at Case Western Reserve University. Faculty members draw upon their own clinical experience and extensive training with such leaders as Jay Haley, Cloé Madanes, Evan Imber-Black, and Robert Shaw, as well as with senior faculty of the Mental Research Institute (MRI) and senior associates of the late Murray Bowen.

The Center utilizes a one-way mirror and videotape equipment to provide live supervision and demonstrations. The approach emphasizes integration of ideas and methods from Structural, Strategic, Transgenerational, and Solution-Focused models. Workshops and seminars are designed for participants at varying levels of prior experience, and range in length from 1- and 2-day workshops to week-long intensives. A year-long externship program is being planned.

CINCINNATI GESTALT INSTITUTE

48 East Hollister
Cincinnati, Ohio 45219
Telephone: 513-421-9739

Year Founded: 1980

Founder(s): Paul Diamond, Ph.D. and Tom Dyehouse, Ph.D., Carol Walk, M.S.W., L.I.S.W.

Accredited by: No accreditation

Affiliated with: None

Psychological Orientation: Gestalt

Duration of Training: 1-year basic training program, 1-year advanced individual therapy practicum

Current Tuition: $1350 for first year and $595 for second year

Seminar Schedule: 3 weekends and 9 1-day classes from October to June

Average Class Size: 12 **Faculty Members:** 3

Annual Applicants: 15

Students Accepted: 12

Enrollment: 12

Graduates: 12

Program Admission Requirements:

Candidates must be members or students of the mental health or counseling professions. Candidates must have a personal interview for admission.

Program Completion Requirements:

Client Requirements: Not applicable

Personal Analysis: Not applicable

Supervision Requirements: Not applicable

Case Presentation Requirements: Not applicable

Thesis Requirements: None

Evaluations: Information not provided

Additional Information:

Cincinnati Gestalt Insitute (CGI) works within a humanistic framework with a foundation in Gestalt Psychology and theory. CGI offers professional training programs, educational seminars, professional supervision, organizational consultation, and introductory and advanced personal growth workshops, as well as individual, couples, and group psychotherapy. CGI's training programs are designed for members and students of the mental health and counseling community, including Psychologists, Social Workers, Nurses, Psychiatrist, Pastoral Counselors, Alcoholism and Chemical Dependency Counselors and Body Therapists.

GESTALT INSTITUTE OF CENTRAL OHIO

3379 East Broad Street
Columbus, Ohio 43213
Telephone: 614-338-1031/Fax: 614-237-9700

Year Founded: 1971

Founder(s): Norman Shub, Robert Timms, and Howard Fink

Accredited by: No accreditation

Affiliated with: None

Psychological Orientation: Gestalt

Duration of Training: 3- year program: for the first 2 years seminars are held 1 Friday a month; third-year trainees choose from various advanced seminars

Current Tuition: $1375 per year for first and second years, $895 for seminars

Application Fee: $100

Miscellaneous Fees: Books and articles

Seminar Schedule: The Gestalt Institute offers a variety of advanced seminars: Child Therapy, Group Therapy, Individual Therapy, and Couples and Marital Therapy. Schedule will vary from year to year.

Average Class Size: 12 **Faculty Members:** 7

Program Admission Requirements:

Candidates must have a master's degree or be in a master's degree program in a helping profession. Prior clinical experience and licensing are helpful, but not required. A personal interview is initially conducted with the Administrative Director, and a second interview with the Clinical Director is required. Submission of a resume and letters of recommendation are required.

Program Completion Requirements:

Seminar Requirements: Trainees must complete 70 class hours per year (10-11 classes, seven hours each). Trainees are required to attend all sessions or make arrangements for makeup at their own expense.

Client Requirements: Not applicable

Personal Analysis: Not applicable

Supervision Requirements: Not applicable

Case Presentation Requirements: Not applicable

Thesis Requirements: None

Evaluations: Information not provided

Additional Information:

The Gestalt approach is rooted in the here and now. The trained Gestalt therapist uses specific therapeutic techniques to work toward completion and bring about change. Students in the Postgraduate Training Program complete a 2-year sequence in Gestalt theory and practice with an emphasis on hands-on work with the Institute's clients. The third year offers advanced seminars in individual therapy and child therapy, as well as intensive work with couples, families, and groups. Trainees often work in small groups to enhance mutual support.

PROCESS WORK CENTER OF PORTLAND

733 NW Everett, Box 11, Suite 3C
Portland, Oregon 97209
Telephone: 503-223-8188/Fax: 503-227-7003

Year Founded: 1990

Founder(s): Dr. Arnold Mindell

Accredited by: State of Oregon, Office of Educational Policy and Planning, OAR 583-30-041

Affiliated with: None

Psychological Orientation: Process-oriented Psychology, also known as Process Work or Dreambody Work.

Duration of Training: 5-year diploma program (at a distance program) and 5-year master's program (residential) leading to MPW (Master of Process Work degree).

Current Tuition: Annual costs including therapy: $4695 minimum, $5985 average, $6405 maximum

Miscellaneous Fees: $250 per year student fees (administrative)

Course Fee: Varies

Seminar Schedule: Students choose a workload of classes and seminars. Average load includes 3 classes per year (48 hours);1 weekly therapy session (1 hour per week); 4 week-long seminars and 4 weekend seminars per year (64 hours); and 1 supervision session per month

Average Class Size: 10-200

Faculty Members: 20

Annual Applicants: 50

Students Accepted: 50

Enrollment: 150

Graduates: 5

Nonenrolled Students: In addition to the classes offered only for registered students, the Institute offers classes that can be taken by both students and the public.

Program Admission Requirements:

Candidates of the diploma program have no academic degree requirement; candidates of the master's program must have a B.A. or B.S., or the equivalent. Candidates must have a personal interview with faculty member(s), receive a written recommendation from interviewer(s), and submit prior transcripts and a curriculum vitae or resume.

Program Completion Requirements:

Seminar Requirements: The number of seminars required is dependent upon individual need, as negotiated with a study committee.

Client Requirements: Students must complete an internship of 420 hours in the public or private sector.

Personal Analysis: Students must complete 250 hours of personal analysis with a Process Work therapist or other approved therapist over 5-year period. Past analysis is not accepted.

Supervision Requirements: Students receive 110 hours of case and therapist supervision during 3- to 5-year period.

Case Presentation Requirements: Case presentations are made on a regular basis.

Thesis Requirements: A research project is required that may take the form of a thesis, article, presentation or performance, demonstrating an ability to apply Process Work.

Evaluations: Evaluation of Phase I (first 2 years of study) consists of 10 40-minute exams covering theoretical, historical, and philosophical components of Process Work. Phase II exams—where students demonstrate their ability to work with their own inner process as well as with couples, individuals, physical symptoms, dreams, groups in conflict, and psychosis—are offered at the end of the 3-year practical phase of training.

Additional Information:

Process Work is an interdisciplinary therapeutic approach to physical symptoms, psychological difficulties, group and relationship conflicts, and other forms of disturbance afflicting individuals and groups. Process Work was initially developed by Arnold Mindell, a Jungian analyst from Zurich, Switzerland, as he explored illness and physical symptoms as meaningful and potentially valuable expressions of the unconscious mind. Process Work now encompasses and integrates Dream Work, Body Work, Communication Theory, Group Process, World Work, Conflict Resolution, and work within our cultures and social structures.

CENTER FOR COGNITIVE THERAPY, UNIVERSITY OF PENNSYLVANIA SCHOOL OF MEDICINE

3600 Market Street
Room 754, The Science Center
Philadelphia, Pennsylvania 19104
Telephone: 215 898-4100/Fax: 215-898-1865

Year Founded: 1975

Founder(s): Aaron T. Beck, M.D.

Accredited by: LCMC Liason Committee on Medical Education, ACGME Accreditation Council for Graduate Medical Education

Affiliated with: University of Pennsylvania School of Medicine

Psychological Orientation: Cognitive therapy

Duration of Training: 1-year postdoctoral fellowship

Current Tuition: None (Fellows receive a stipend)

Seminar Schedule: Approximately 3 hours of seminars per week, 2 hours of group supervision per week, and 3 hours of individual supervision per week.

Average Class Size: 5

Faculty Members: 15

Annual Applicants: 30

Students Accepted: 4

Enrollment: 4

Graduates: 4

Nonenrolled Students: Professionals and non-professionals are permitted to take classes.

Program Admission Requirements:

A Ph.D. in Clinical or Counseling Psychology is preferred but not required for admission. Candidates must have at least 1 year of clinical internship. A curriculum vitae, 3 letters of recommendation, an application form, an audiotape or videotape of role-played or actual therapy session, transcripts, and a letter of interest are required.

Program Completion Requirements:

Seminar Requirements: Candidates must complete 4 hours of seminars per week.

Client Requirements: Candidates must conduct 20 client sessions per week, plus 2 intake interviews.

Personal Analysis: Not applicable

Supervision Requirements: Candidates receive 3 hours of individual supervision and 2 hours of group supervision each week for 1 year.

Case Presentation Requirements: Case presentations are given by candidates approximately once every month.

Thesis Requirements: None

Evaluations: Written evaluations are done by each supervisor (2 per year).

FAMILY INSTITUTE OF PHILADELPHIA

1527 Brandywine Street
Philadelphia, Pennsylvania 19130-4002
Telephone: 215-567-1396

Year Founded: 1964

Founder(s): J. Jungreis, J. Framo, G. Grossman, A. Friedman, G. Spark, O. Weiner, R. Speck, I. Nagy, O. Pollack, J. Sonne, M. Griffel, R. Weiner, D. Rubenstein

Accredited by: American Association of Marriage and Family Therapy

Affiliated with: None

Psychological Orientation: All major models of Family Therapy

Duration of Training: 3 years/part-time

Current Tuition: $2,400 per year

Application Fee: $35

Seminar Schedule: First Year—Wednesdays 7 P.M.-9 P.M.; Second Year — Tuesdays 7:30 P.M. to 9:30 P.M.; Third Year—Thursdays 7 P.M.-9 P.M.

Average Class Size: 20

Faculty Members: 59

Annual Applicants: 28

Students Accepted: 16

Enrollment: 16

Graduates: 12

Nonenrolled Students: The Institute allows professionals to take certain classes occasionally and nonprofessionals to take Introductory classes. No one is permitted to audit classes.

Program Admission Requirements:

Candidates must have a master's degree in a related profession. Some prior clinical experience is preferred. Certification/licensing is required if candidates are using private practice cases for supervision. Candidates must submit an official transcript, 2 letters of recommendation, a current resume, and be interviewed by 2 faculty members.

Program Completion Requirements:

Seminar Requirements: One seminar is required each clinical year, from September through June.

Client Requirements: Candidates must conduct 500 client sessions, registered and supervised by FIP. Of these, 350 sessions are on-site in a clinic run by FIP.

Personal Analysis: Not applicable

Supervision Requirements: Not applicable

Case Presentation Requirements: Formal case presentations are made for supervision at the end of the second and third years.

Thesis Requirements: None

Evaluations: Supervisors evaluate clinical skills as well as the use of concepts in practice. Papers and case presentations evaluate the candidate's ability to apply theoretical concepts.

Additional Information:

The Training Program of The Family Institute of Philadelphia is a part-time, flexible program. The mission of The Family Institute of Philadelphia, which is a professional organization as well as the training program, is to increase and support knowledge and skill in practice of Family Therapy. The Program is primarily clinical. It teaches all major models of Family Therapy. Experts in each model are represented on the faculty and supervisory staff. The goal of the program is to produce strong flexible therapists who have chosen the model or models that work best for them.

INSTITUTE FOR PSYCHOANALYTIC PSYCHOTHERAPIES

26 Summit Grove Avenue, Suite 217
Bryn Mawr, Pennsylvania 19010
Telephone: 215-752-7997

Accredited by: National Association for the Advancement of Psychoanalysis (NAAP), American Board for the Accreditation of Psychoanalysis

Affiliated with: None

Psychological Orientation: Freudian Psychotherapies including Classical, Object Relations, and Ego Psychology

Duration of Training: 3 years

Current Tuition: $125 per credit for 30 credits

Application Fee: $35

Supervision Fee: $50 per hour

Miscellaneous Fees: $50 annual matriculation fee

Seminar Schedule: Seminars meet for 25 hours (10 sessions) on Saturdays. There are 2 seminars each trimester for 3 years for a total of 18 seminars (450 seminar hours).

Average Class Size: 7

Faculty Members: 11

Annual Applicants: 10

Students Accepted: 7

Enrollment: 7

Graduates: 5

Program Admission Requirements:

Candidates must have a master's degree, a doctoral degree, or an M.D. No prior experience is required. Prior certification is not required, but it is recommended. A personal interview, essay, 3 recomendations, and transcripts are required for admission.

Program Completion Requirements:

Seminar Requirements: Candidates must complete 18 seminars (30 hours each).

Client Requirements: Candidates must work with 4 clients and a minimum of 3 supervisors. Payment for clients treated is used to defray supervision costs.

Personal Analysis: Candidates are required to have 300 hours of personal analysis. Past analysis may be accepted.

Supervision Requirements: Candidates are required to complete 100 hours of supervision with 3 control cases.

Case Presentation Requirements: Case presentations are made during ongoing seminars for 2 years.

Thesis Required: A thesis is required.

Evaluations: Evaluations are conducted by a committee chosen by the candidate.

MARRIAGE COUNCIL OF PHILADELPHIA

4025 Chestnut Street
Philadelphia, Pennsylvania 19104
Telephone: 215-382-6680/Fax: 215-386-1743

Year Founded: 1932

Founder(s): Emily Mudd, Ph.D.

Accredited by: A.A.M.F.T.

Affiliated with: University of Pennsylvania School of Medicine

Psychological Orientation: Intersystem—a comprehensive and integrative approach to treatment

Duration of Training: 1 year full-time, 2 to 4 years part-time

Current Tuition: $9300 full-time, part-time varies

Seminar Schedule: 10 classes (most meet in the morning)

Average Class Size: 20 **Faculty Members:** 40

Annual Applicants: 70 **Students Accepted:** 20

Enrollment: 50 **Graduates:** 15

Nonenrolled Students: Most professionals apply for course work only, and hold a clinical degree.

Program Admission Requirements:

Candidates must have a minimum of a master's in a clinical area. One year of clinical experience is required. Prior certification or licensing is preferred. Letters of recommendation, an autobiographical statement, and a personal interview are required for admission.

Program Completion Requirements:

Seminar Requirements: Candidates must complete 10 seminar classes.

Client Requirements: Candidates must conduct a minimum of 500 clinical hours.

Personal Analysis: Personal analysis is not required

Supervision Requirements: Candidates must have a minimum of 200 hours of supervision each year for the duration of the program.

Case Presentation Requirements: One case must be presented each week. Videotape supervision is conducted.

Thesis Requirements: None

Evaluations: There is a mid-training evaluation of clinical progress and semester progress reports from the supervisors.

Additional Information:

In continuous operation since 1932, the Marriage Council is the pioneering center for the treatment of relationships. In 1948, the training program was established to train advanced clinicians in Marital, Couple, Family, and Sex Therapy. The program offers 2 unique educational advantages. First, it is 1 of the 14 freestanding training institutes nationally that is accredited by A.A.M.F.T. Second, it is the operational unit of the Division of Family Study in the Department of Psychiatry at the University of Pennsylvania School of Medicine.

MILTON H. ERICKSON INSTITUTE OF PHILADELPHIA

Rosemont Plaza, Suite 8
1062 Lancaster Avenue
Rosemont, Pennsylvania
Telephone: 215-525-0223

Year Founded: 1985

Founder(s): Dr. John Edgette and Dr. Janet Edgette

Accredited by: No accreditation

Affiliated with: The Milton H. Erickson Foundation, Phoenix

Psychological Orientation: Ericksonian Hypnosis and Psychotherapy, NLP, Brief Therapy

Duration of Training: Up to 2 years

Current Tuition: Approximately $450 per 15-week course

Seminar Schedule: Fundamentals and intermediate course segments are 2 hours per week for 15 weeks. Advanced and case supervision segments are 2 hours every 2 weeks for 10 weeks.

Average Class Size: 5-6

Faculty Members: 2

Annual Applicants: 15

Students Accepted: 15

Enrollment: 15

Nonenrolled Students: A minimum of a master's degree in the mental health sciences is required to take classes at the Institute. Individual arrangements can be made to suit various professionals' needs.

Program Admission Requirements:

Candidates must have a minimum of a master's degree in the mental health sciences or be graduate students in mental health.

Program Completion Requirements:

Seminar Requirements: Participants can choose to take as many or as few course segments as they like. There is no graduation per se, but the Institute does offer letters of completion (4 courses required).

Client Requirements: Not applicable

Personal Analysis: Not applicable

Supervision Requirements: Not applicable

Case Presentation Requirements: As desired by participant

Thesis Requirements: None

Evaluations: Information not provided

Additional Information:

The Milton H. Erickson Institute of Philidelphia is a private facility offering clinical services and professional training in Ericksonian Hypnosis and Psychotherapy. Training is conducted by the co-directors Drs. John and Janet Edgette, each of whom has been on the faculty of recent international congresses on Ericksonian approaches to Hypnosis and Psychotherapy. The format of training at the Institute is small group instruction with a strong experiential emphasis. Classes consist of lecture, videos, case studies, case supervision, demonstrations, group inductions, and experiential exercises.

PHILADELPHIA SCHOOL OF PSYCHOANALYSIS

1331 Pine Street
Philadelphia, Pennsylvania 19107
Telephone:

Year Founded: 1971

Founder(s): Dr. Harold R. Stern

Accredited by: NAAP in 1975

Affiliated with: None

Psychological Orientation: Psychoanalysis

Duration of Training: Varies (usually takes several years beyond the completion of 4 years of course work)

Application Fee: $25

Course Fee: $175 per course (3 courses per semester)

Seminar Schedule: 3 classes per semester, 1 1/2 hours, Saturday 8:50 A.M. to 2:20 P.M.

Average Class Size: 14

Faculty Members: 20

Annual Applicants: 36

Students Accepted: 24

Enrollment: 120

Graduates: 53

Nonenrolled Students: Preclinical courses are open to nonprofessionals as well as professionals.

Program Admission Requirements:

Candidates must have a master's degree. Candidates are accepted with no prior clinical experience, but are not permitted to see patients in PSP's clinic until 1 year of class and supervision is completed. Candidates must have personal interviews, submit application forms and names for recommendation, and visit to observe the school and classes.

Program Completion Requirements:

Seminar Requirements: Candidates must complete 28 courses.

Client Requirements: Candidates must complete 500 hours of approved client sessions.

Personal Analysis: Candidates must complete a minimum of 300 hours of personal analysis with an approved Modern Analyst. Past analysis with an approved analyst is accepted.

Supervision Requirements: Candidates receive a minimum of 100 hours of supervision.

Case Presentation Requirements: Candidates present 7 cases and give a final case presentation.

Thesis Requirements: Candidates must complete a final paper; a previously completed paper may be accepted.

Evaluations: Evaluations are based on course work, case presentation, final paper, theory exam, and final case presentation.

Additional Information:

PSP's academic activities are carried on in 2 Philadelphia locations. Regular classes are held on Saturdays during the academic year at Drexel University. In addition, PSP owns the premises at 313 South 16th Street, occupied by its clinic, the Philadelphia Consultation Center, where students are provided with office facilities for the treatment of private patients. The clinic functions are under student direction and its services are open to the public.

Advancement through the Training Program is guided by evaluation of the candidate's progress enabling him/her to coordinate the results of the training analysis and complete coursework with the commencement of his/her supervised practice.

WESTERN PENNSYLVANIA FAMILY CENTER

733 North Highland Avenue
Pittsburgh, Pennsylvania 15206
Telephone: 412-362-2295

Year Founded: 1985

Founder(s): Paulina G. McCullough, M.S.W., James B. Smith, M.S., Cynthia Larkby, M.S.W., A.C.S.W., Stuart E. Liebman, M.D., Walter H. Smith, Ph.D., and Anne Vogeding Read, M.A.

Accredited by: No accreditation

Affiliated with: None

Psychological Orientation: Bowen Family Systems Theory

Duration of Training: Varies from 2-day workshops to a core-curriculum program of 2 academic semesters

Current Tuition: Courses are individually priced

Application Fee: Varies **Registration Fee:** Varies

Seminar Schedule: Core program is held on Tuesdays from 5 P.M.-8:15 P.M.

Average Class Size: Varies from 5 to more than 120

Faculty Members: 10

Program Admission Requirements:

For the Postgraduate course, candidates must demonstrate a serious interest in studying Family Functioning.

Program Completion Requirements:

Client Requirements: Not applicable

Personal Analysis: Not applicable

Supervision Requirements: Not applicable

Case Presentation Requirements: Not applicable

Thesis Requirements: None

Evaluations: Information not provided

Additional Information:

The Western Pennsylvania Family Center is a private, nonprofit organization committed to providing training and education in the study of Family and Individual Functioning for personal, professional or clinical purposes. Since 1985, the Family Center has been offering educational programming that is designed to enhance services provided by both the professional and lay community that serve families in educational, medical, clinical, religious, and social service agencies and institutions.

MILTON H. ERICKSON INSTITUTE OF AUSTIN

605 Baylor
Austin, Texas 78703
Telephone: 512-479-0455/Fax: 512-479-0455

Year Founded: 1988

Founder(s): Seyma Calibman, C.S.W./A.C.P. and George Glaser, C.S.W.\A.C.P.

Accredited by: The Milton H. Erickson Foundation, Phoenix

Affiliated with: The Milton H. Erickson Institutes of Texas

Psychological Orientation: Ericksonian Psychotherapy and Hypnosis

Duration of Training: 1 year seminars (56 hours of instruction), weekend workshops, 6-session short courses

Current Tuition: $895; $950 (in installments) for 1-year semester

Registration Fee: $150

Supervision Fee: $90

Seminar Schedule: Five hours, once per month (12 classes per year) for the year -long training. These begin in October and in April. For other courses, please write and request a schedule.

Average Class Size: 10

Faculty Members: 4

Annual Applicants: 21

Students Accepted: 20

Enrollment: 20

Graduates: 0

Nonenrolled Students: The Institute will create classes for professionals or graduate students, but will not open ongoing classes to occasional students.

Program Admission Requirements:

Candidates must have a master's degree or a doctorate in mental health or health; graduate students in mental health also are admitted. If no hypnosis is taught, a bachelor's degree in a mental health field is acceptable.

Program Completion Requirements:

Seminar Requirements: Students attend on a class-by-class basis.

Client Requirements: Not applicable

Personal Analysis: Not applicable

Supervision Requirements: Candidates must fulfill the regular requirements for licensing/certification.

Case Presentation Requirements: One hour of consultation is offered each month as part of the 5-hour class. Students are not required to present, but may request consultation.

Thesis Requirements: None

Evaluations: The faculty observes students on an ongoing basis and gives feedback. No formal evaluations are required.

Additional Information:

The Milton H. Erickson Institute of Austin provides professional training in Ericksonian Psychotherapy and Hypnosis, with application to specific client populations. Two of the Institute's faculty work with children using Ericksonian approaches, and one faculty memeber uses art therapy as a trance-inducing medium. The Institute also brings presenters to Texas for a variety of events designed to meet the needs of practitioners of all skill levels.

The Institute believes that therapists must remain true to their own personalities and styles. It strives, therefore, to offer training that facilitates integration and personal evolution, using gentleness, respect for clients, and humor to promote therapeutic change.

MILTON H. ERICKSON INSTITUTE OF HOUSTON

2012 Bissonnet
Houston, Texas 77005
Telephone: 713-529-4589

Year Founded: 1987

Founder(s): Carol J. Kershaw, Ed.D., and J. William Wade, M.Div., L.P.C.

Accredited by: Milton H. Erickson Foundation, Phoenix

Affiliated with: Milton H. Erickson Institutes of Texas

Psychological Orientation: Ericksonian, Strategic, Systemic

Duration of Training: Both introductory and advanced programs are 10 months long.

Current Tuition: $1200 per 10 months

Application Fee: $25

Registration Fee: $300

Seminar Schedule: Both introductory and advanced programs meet 1 Friday each month for 5 hour (12 P.M. to 5 P.M.), September through June.

Average Class Size: 18

Faculty Members: 4

Annual Applicants: 30

Students Accepted: 25

Enrollment: 25

Graduates: 22

Nonenrolled Students: The Institute sponsors occasional weekend seminars for professionals who want a brief exposure to Ericksonian psychotherapy.

Program Admission Requirements:

Candidates must have a master's degree in Psychology or a related field, or be enrolled in a graduate program. Candidates must have completed a practicum if they are at the graduate level. Candidates must have a licence in Medicine, Nursing, Psychology, Counseling, Social Work, or Family Therapy, or be in supervision. A complete application and 2 letters of recommendation are required for admission.

Program Completion Requirements:

Seminar Requirements: Candidates are required to complete 10 classes (45 continuing education hours)

Client Requirements: Not applicable

Personal Analysis: Not applicable

Supervision Requirements: Not applicable

Case Presentation Requirements: Monthly case presentations are included in the program.

Thesis Requirements: None

Evaluations: Information not provided

Additional Information:

The Milton H. Erickson Institute of Houston is an educational and training institute that has as its purpose the promotion and advancement of Ericksonian approaches to hypnosis and psychotherapy. Milton H. Erickson, M.D. (1901-1980) was a pioneer in the fields of Clinical Hypnosis and Strategic Psychotherapy. His innovative and unique style of therapy attracted the attention of Gregory Bateson, Aldous Huxley, and Margaret Mead. Erickson's approach was both unconventional and pragmatic, and his influence is evident in such diverse treatment approaches as Individual Psychotherapy, Marital Therapy, Sex Therapy, and Family Therapy, as well as Clinical Hypnosis.

The Milton H. Erickson Institute of Houston is dedicated to the belief that psychotherapy is most effective when it is tailored to the individuals and families in treatment and is respectful of each person's uniqueness and individuality. The faculty of the Institute is multidisciplinary with backgrounds in Psychiatry, Psychology, Social Work, Nursing, and Family Therapy.

The institute is affiliated with the Milton H. Erickson Institutes of Texas located in Houston, Austin, and Dallas and is licensed by the Milton H. Erickson Foundation in Phoenix, Arizona.

FAMILY INSTITUTE OF VIRGINIA, INC

2910 Monument Avenue
Richmond, Virginia 23221
Telephone: 804-355-6876

Year Founded: 1977

Founder(s): Joan E. Winter

Accredited by: No accreditation

Affiliated with: College of William and Mary, Harry Aponte, Virginia Satir, Murray Bowen, and Milton H. Erickson

Psychological Orientation: Family systems

Duration of Training: 9-month clinical time

Current Tuition: $3500 per 9 month training program

Application Fee: $500

Seminar Schedule: 11 hours per 9 month program

Average Class Size: 12

Faculty Members: 2

Annual Applicants: 50

Students Accepted: 25

Enrollment: 25

Graduates: 250

Program Admission Requirements:

A graduate degree in a mental health field, organizational development, or a medical field. A personal interview and a curriculum vitae are required for admission.

Program Completion Requirements:

Seminar Requirements: Attendence at the 9 monthly 2-day seminars is required.

Client Requirements: Not applicable

Personal Analysis: Not applicable

Supervision Requirements: Not applicable

Case Presentation Requirements: Candidates must make a minimum of 3 in-depth presentations.

Thesis Requirements: None

Evaluations: Information not provided

Additional Information:

The Person and Practice of the Therapist is an intensive course designed for experienced clinicians under the auspices of The Family Institute of Virginia. The context is a small group of up to 14 members. This format facilitates a high level of professional competence, trust, and personal participation. Such training primarily helps the therapist to know himself in the "therapeutic context" and to learn to use his personal attitudes, characteristics and experiences in his or her work with patients. Various teaching modalities are utilized, including supervision of live treatment sessions, oral and videotape critiques of work conducted by each therapist in his own practice setting, *in vivo* role-playing, and feedback from both trainer and group members regarding each clinician's practice and personal impact. In the process, the clinician will learn to recognize and monitor his or her personal reactions while conducting therapy. The practitioner also will learn to manage and use positive and negative feelings in developing his/her professional skills vis-à-vis the client's personal, cultural, ethnic, political, and religious beliefs.

VIRGINIA ERICKSONIAN INSTITUTE

Randolph-Macon College
Ashland, Virgina 23005
Telephone: 804-752-7270/Fax: 804-752-7231

Year Founded: 1984

Founder(s): Drs. Russell A. Bourne, Jr., Robert N. Glenn, Malcom M. Hart, and Charles S. McGhee

Accredited by: Randolph-Macon College

Affiliated with: Randolph-Macon College, Milton H. Erickson Foundation, Phoenix

Psychological Orientation: Ericksonian approaches to Hypnosis and Psychotherapy, Strategic and Hypnotic approaches to Brief Therapy

Duration of Training: Varies

Current Tuition: Varies

Seminar Schedule: Varies

Average Class Size: 30

Faculty Members: 4

Nonenrolled Students: Professionals may take occasional classes.

Program Admission Requirements:

Candidates must be mental health or health care professionals, or educators with graduate degrees from accredited institutions (Ph.D., M.D., M.S.W., M.A., etc.)

Program Completion Requirements:

Client Requirements: Not applicable

Personal Analysis: Not applicable

Supervision Requirements: Not applicable

Case Presentation Requirements: Not applicable

Thesis Requirements: None

Evaluations: Information not provided

Additional Information:

The Virginia Ericksonian Institute (VEI) is a nonprofit, educational corporation located at Randolph-Macon College. An official chapter of the Milton H. Erickson Foundation in Phoenix. VEI is committed to the training of health care professionals and educators in Ericksonian approaches to Hypnosis and Psychotherapy. The philosophy of the Ericksonian approach is predicated on a deep appreciation for the uniqueness of each individual and a profound respect for the capacity of one's personal resources. Treatment and education emphasizes cooperating with and utilizing conscious and unconscious psychological, biological, behavioral processes to facilitate adjustment and change. In addition to their regular program of training, VEI welcomes the opportunity to provide consultation, supervision, and individually designed training programs for mental health and health care professionals and/or agencies.

GEORGETOWN FAMILY CENTER

4400 MacArthur Boulevard, NW
Washington, D.C. 20007
Telephone: 202-965-0730

Accredited by: No accreditation

Affiliated with: None

Psychological Orientation: Bowen Theory

Duration of Training: Open ended, 3 years minimum

Current Tuition: $2,500 **Application Fee:** $35

Seminar Schedule: Special Postgraduate Program is 4 years long, 21 hour-long sessions in Washington, D.C.; Regular Postgraduate is 3 years, 15 hours weekly for 32 weeks. Community Course is 2 hours biweekly for 18 weeks.

Average Class Size: SPG is 20; RPG is 5; Community course is 15.

Faculty Members: 8

Annual Applicants: 5

Students Accepted: 4

Enrollment: 17

Graduates: 4

Nonenrolled Students: Professionals and nonprofessionals may take, but not audit, classes.

Program Admission Requirements:

Candidates must have completed academic and graduate training. Prior clinical experience is useful, but not required. Candidates must have finished personal psychotherapy, if any, before entering programs. Candidates must complete the Family Center application with an essay and have an interview when the applicant is local.

Program Completion Requirements:

Client Requirements: Not applicable

Personal Analysis: Not applicable

Supervision Requirements: Not applicable

Case Presentation Requirements: Not applicable

Thesis Requirements: None

Evaluations: Information not provided

GESTALT PSYCHOTHERAPY CENTER

1834 Swann St. N.W.
Washington, D.C. 20009
Telephone: 202-662-6425

Year Founded: 1976

Founder(s): Rudolph Bauer Ph.D., and Shanon Bauer, M.S.W.

Accredited by: Continuing Education Credit from Maryland Psychological Association, category A accreditation.

Affiliated with: None

Psychological Orientation: Gestalt Psychotherapy in an Object Relations context

Duration of Training: 2 years

Current Tuition: $1080 per year

Seminar Schedule: Nine days a year (3 hours a year)

Average Class Size: 25 **Faculty Members:** 12

Annual Applicants: 70 **Students Accepted:** 20

Program Admission Requirements:

Candidates must have a Ph.D., M.D., or M.S.W. Candidates must have completed an internship. Candidates must be licensed in their profession. Candidates must have completed, or be receiving, personal psychotherapy. A personal interview is required.

Program Completion Requirements:

Client Requirements: Not applicable

Personal Analysis: Not applicable

Supervision Requirements: Not applicable

Case Presentation Requirements: Not applicable

Thesis Requirements: None

Evaluations: Information not provided

FAMILY SERVICE OF MILWAUKEE

2819 West Highland Boulevard
Milwaukee, Wisconsin 53208
Telephone: 414-342-4560/Fax: 414-342-5326

Year Founded: 1972

Founder(s): Jeanne Robinson, Ph.D., Insoo Berg, M.S.W., Ramona Hietpas, M.S.W., David Hoffman, M.A.

Accredited by: Commission on Accreditation of the American Association for Marriage and Family Therapy

Affiliated with: Family Service America, Family Service of Milwaukee

Psychological Orientation: Family Systems, Structural/Solution-focused, Object Relations

Duration of Training: 2 years

Current Tuition: $3600 first year, $3000 second year

Application Fee: $40 **Supervision Fee:** $200

Seminar Schedule: 7 seminars of 30 to 96 hours for a total of 336 hours

Average Class Size: 12 **Faculty Members:** 14

Annual Applicants: 22 **Students Accepted:** 12

Enrollment: 12 **Graduates:** 5

Nonenrolled Students: All seminars and workshops are available to professionals in mental health or Marriage and Family Therapy.

Program Admission Requirements:

Candidates must have a master's degree or Ph.D. in a mental health field or an M.D. Neither prior clinical experience nor prior licensing are required. A curriculum vitae, transcripts, 2 letters of recommendation, and 2 interviews are required for admission.

Program Completion Requirements:

Seminar Requirements: Candidates are required to complete 7 seminars (336 class hours).

Client Requirements: Candidates are required to conduct 1000 client sessions for the Family Counselor Program, and 500 client sessions for the Adjunct Counselor Program. Clients fall into a full range of diagnostic categories and case modalities (child, individual adult, couples, families, groups).

Personal Analysis: No personal analysis is required.

Supervision Requirements: Candidates must receive 350 to 460 hours of supervision over a 2-year period. 75 to 150 client sessions are required for control cases.

Case Presentation Requirements: Weekly case presentations are required.

Thesis Requirements: None

Evaluations: Counselor-trainees are evaluated at screening and every 6 months on a competency-based scale measuring progress on skills in assessment, case management, applying family theory, use of self, and therapeutic communication skills. Trainees also demonstrate competency through specially designed projects during each year of the program.

Additional Information:

The Family Therapy Training Institute is one of the first accredited marriage and family therapy programs. It offers an intensive, competency-based program designed to meet requirements for AAMFT membership and Wisconsin MFT certification for post-master trainees. The Institute staff includes 10 AAMFT-approved supervisors, who teach cutting-edge seminars on family systems, structural and Solution-focused Therapy, Ethics, Family Assessment, and Advanced Family Theory.

The majority of supervision is done in live one-way mirror group settings. FTTI is housed in Wisconsin's oldest and largest nonprofit, nonsectarian social services agency, Family Services of Milwaukee, which has a multicultural staff and serves clients from all socioeconomic, cultural, and diagnostic groups in four clinics throughout Milwaukee.

APPENDIX
Institutes Listed by Subspecialty

ADLERIAN

The Americas Institute of Adlerian Studies

BODY THERAPY

Center for Reichian Energetic Therapy
Grof Transpersonal Training
Hartford Family Institute
Integrative Body Psychotherapy of Boulder
Institute of Core Energetics
Rosenberg -Rand Institute of Integrative Body Psychotherapy
Rosen Center Northeast
University for Humanistic Studies

BRIEF THERAPY

American Hypnosis Training Academy, Inc.
Center for Family & Brief Therapies
Family Therapy Institute of Provident Counseling, Inc.
Family Therapy Institute of Santa Barbara
Mental Research Institute
Milton H. Erickson Foundation, Inc.
Milton H. Erickson Institute of Northern Illinois
Milton H. Erickson of San Diego
New England Institute for NLP
Virginia Ericksonian Institute

COGNITIVE-BEHAVIORAL

Boston Center for Rational Emotive Therapy
Center for Cognitive Therapy, University of Penn
Center for Family & Brief Therapies
Family Therapy Institute of Santa Barbara
Forest Institute of Professional Psychology
Institute for Integrative Psychotherapy
Institute for Rational-Emotive Therapy

DEGREE-GRANTING

California Family Study Center
California Institute of Integral Studies
Forest Institute of Professional Psychology
Institute for Modern Psychoanalysis
Institute of Transpersonal Psychology
Reformed Theological Institute
University for Humanistic Studies

ECLECTIC

Forest Institute of Professional Psychology

MARRIAGE, FAMILY, & CHILDREN

Blanton-Peale Graduate Institute
California Family Study Center
California School of Professional Psychology
Center for Family & Brief Therapies
Center for Family Consultation
Center for Family Learning
Center for Family & Psychological Studies
Child and Adolescent Psychotherapy Training Program
Family Institute of Philadelphia
Family Institute of Virginia, Inc.
Family Institute of Westchester
Family Service of Milwaukee
Family Therapy Insitute, Inc.

Family Therapy Institute of Provident Counsel
Family Therapy Insitute of Santa Barbara
Family Therapy Institute of Southern New Hampshire
Georgetown Family Center
Integrative Body Psychotherapy of Boulder
Long Island Insititute of Psychoanalysis
Marriage Council of Philadephia
Mental Research Institute
Milton H. Erickson Institute of Northern Illinois
Minnesota Institute of Family Dynamics
New Hope Guild Centers Training Programs
Psychoanalytic Institute of the Postgraduate Center for Mental Health
Reformed Theological Institute
Rosenberg -Rand Institute of Integrative Body Psychotherapy
Violet Oaklander Institute
Western Pennsylvania Family Center

GESTALT

Cincinnati Gestalt Institute
Gestalt Center of Long Island
Gestalt Institute of Central Florida
Gestalt Institute of Central Ohio
Gestalt Institute of Phoenix
Gestalt Institute of San Francisco
Gestalt Psychotherapy Center
Gestalt Therapy Center of Baltimore
Gestalt Therapy Center of Queens
Gestalt Therapy Institute of Los Angeles
Gestalt Training Center - Boone, NC
Hartford Family Institute
Indianapolis Gestalt Institute
Rosenberg- Rand Institute of Integrative Body Psychotherapy

GROUP

Boston Institute for Psychotherapy, Inc.
Center for the Advancement of Group Studies
Hartford Family Institute
Psychodrama Training Institute
Psychoanalytic Institute of the Postgraduate Center for Mental Health

HYPNOTHERAPY

American Hypnosis Training Academy, Inc.
Hypnosis Clearing House
Maryland Institute for Ericksonian Hypnosis & Psychotherapy
Milton H. Erickson Foundation, Inc.
Milton H. Erickson Institute of Austin
Milton H. Erickson Institute of Houston
Milton H. Erickson Institute of New Jersey
Milton H. Erickson Institute of Northern Illinois
Milton H. Erickson Institute of San Diego
Milton H. Erickson Institute of Philadelphia
New England Institute for NLP
Virginia Ericksonian Institute

JUNGIAN

Avalon Institute
C.G. Jung Institute of Los Angeles
C.G. Jung Institute of New York

PSYCHO-SPIRITUAL

California Institute of Integral Studies
Family Therapy Institute of Santa Barbara
Grof Transpersonal Training
Hartford Family Institute
New England Institute of NLP
Psychological Studies Institute
Reformed Theological Institute

PSYCHOANALYSIS

Advanced Institute for Analytic Psychotherapy
Avalon Institute
Blanton-Peale Graduate Institute
Boston Center for Modern Psychoanalytic Studies Inc.

California School of Professional Psychology
Center for the Advancement of Group Studies
Center for Modern Psychoanalytic Studies
Center for Psychoanalytic Study
C.G. Jung Institute of New York
Chicago Center for Psychoanalysis
Child and Adolescent Psychotherapy Training Program
Colorado Center for Modern Psych Studies
Greenwich Institute for Psychoanalytic Studies
Institute for Contemporary Psychotherapy
Institute for Expressive Analysis
Institute for Modern Psychoanalysis
Institute for Psychoanalysis
Institute for Psychoanalysis of Chicago
Institute for Psychoanalytic Psychoatherapies
Institute for Psychoanalysis & Psychotherapy of N.J.
IPTAR
L.A. Institute & Society for Psychoanalytic Studies
Long Island Institute of Psychoanalysis
Manhattan Institute for Psychoanaylsis
Masschusetts Institute for Psychoanalysis
Masterson Institute
Metropolitan Institute for Training in Psychoanalytic Psychotherapy
National Institute for the Psychotherapies
New Hope Guild Centers Training Program
New Jersey Institute for Training in Psychoanalysis
New York Freudian Society
New York Psychoanalytic Institute
New York School for Psychoanalytic Psychotherapy
Philadelphia School of Psychoanalysis
Psychoanalytic Institute of New England
Psychoanalytic Institute of the Postgraduate Center for Mental Health
Psychoanalytic Training Institute of the NY Counseling & Guidance Service
Rosenberg -Rand Institute of Integrative Body Psychotherapy
Training Institute of the N.P.A.P.
Washington Square Institute for Psychotherapy and Mental Health
Westchester Center for the Study of Psychoanalysis & Psychotherapy
Westchester Institute for Training in Psychoanalysis & Psychotherapy
Women's Therapy Centre Institute

PSYCHOTHERAPY

Advanced Institute for Analytic Psychotherapy
Blanton-Peale Graduate Institute
Boston Institute for Psychotherapy, Inc.
California Family Study Center
California Institute for Clinical Social Work
California Institute for Integral Studies
California School of Professional Psychology
Center for Family & Psychological Studies
Center for Reichian Energetic Therapy
Child and Adolescent Psychotherapy Training Program
Cincinnati Gestalt Institute
Family Service of Milawaukee
Family Therapy Institute of Santa Barbara
Forest Institute of Professional Psychology
Gestalt Institute of Central Florida
Gestalt Institute of Central Ohio
Gestalt Center of Long Island
Gestalt Institute of San Francisco
Gestalt Psychotherapy Center
Gestalt Therapy Center of Baltimore
Gestalt Training Center - Boone, N.C.
Gestalt Therapy Center of Queens
Gestalt Therapy Institute of Los Angeles
Greenwich Institute for Psychoanayltic Studies
Hartford Family Institute
Institute for Contemporary Psychotherapy
Institute of Core Energetics
Institute for Diagogical Psychotherapy
Institute for Expressive Analysis
Institute for Integrative Psychotehrapy
Institute for Psychoanalysis
Institute for Psychoanalysis & Psychotherapy of N.J.
Institute of Sports Psychology
Integrative Body Psychotherapy of Boulder
Long Island Institute of Psychoanaylsis
Maryland Institute for Ericksonian Hypnosis & Psychotherapy
Masterson Institute
Mental Research Institute
Metropolitan Institute for Training in Psychoanalytic Psychotherapy
Milton H. Erickson Foundation, Inc.

Milton H. Erickson Institute of Austin
Milton H. Erickson Institute of Houston
Milton H. Erickson Institute of New Jersey
Milton H. Erickson Institute of Northern Illinois
Milton H. Erickson Institute of Philadelphia
National Institute for the Psychotherapies
New York School for Psychoanalytic Psychotherapy
The Person Centered Expressive Therapy Institute
Psychodrama Training Institute
Psychoanalytic Institute of the Postgraduate Center for Mental Health
Psychoanalytic Training Institute of the NY Counseling & Guidance Service
Psychological Studies Institute
Synthesis Center
Violet Oaklander Institute
Virginia Ericksonian Institute
Washington Square Institute for Psychology and Mental Health
Westchester Center for the Study of Psychoanalysis & Psychotherapy

TRANSPERSONAL

Grof Transpersonal Training
Huntington Therapy Institute
Hypnosis Clearing House
Institute of Sports Psychology
Institute of Transpersonal Psychology
New England Institute for NLP
The Person Centered Expressive Therapy Institute
Rosen Center Northeast
Synthesis Center
University for Humanistic Studies

Help Us Update Our Next Edition

Please let us know if you have any comments or corrections for this edition. If you feel that we should add an institute, please send us their name and address and we will send them a questionnaire.

If we use the information that you supply, you will receive a complimentary copy of the next edition.

Comments/Corrections:

Please send an institute questionnaire to:

My name and address:

Please return this page (or fax a copy) to:
Laurie A. Baum
National Directory Update
Brunner/Mazel Publishers
19 Union Square West
New York, NY 10003
Fax: (212) 242-6339